CULTURES OF THE WORLD®

ALBANIA

Mary Lee Knowlton

BENCHMARK BOOKS

MARSHALL CAVENDISH
NEW YORK

PICTURE CREDITS
Cover: © Bill Foley/Bruce Coleman©www.bciusa.com
Albanian Tennis Federation: 115 • AFP: 11 • alt.TYPE/REUTERS: 36, 41, 42, 54, 55, 57, 58, 64,
73, 77, 109, 111, 112, 113, 122, 123, 124, 127 • ANA Press Agency: 23, 71, 128 • Bes Stock: 8,
13, 14, 15, 17, 19, 45, 83, 99 • Focus Team Italy: 4, 5, 21, 47, 48, 70, 76, 78, 93, 103, 116, 129
• Corbis Inc.: 1, 3, 7, 10, 18, 20, 22, 25, 27, 29, 30, 33, 34, 35, 38, 39, 43, 44, 46, 49, 50, 56, 63,
66, 68, 69, 72, 74, 80, 81, 82, 84, 85, 86, 91, 94, 96, 97, 100, 104, 105, 106, 107, 108, 110, 117, 118,
120, 121, 126 • Susie M. Eisling/Stockfood: 131 • Robert Elsie/wwwalbanianliterature.com: 92
• HBL Network Photo Agency: 6, 9, 12, 28, 40, 89, 90, 102 • Milutin Milosevic, World Scout
Bureau: 119 • North Wind Picture Archives: 24, 26 • Studio Bonisolli/Stockfood: 130 • Sylvia
Cordaiy Photo Library: 16, 51, 52, 53, 60, 98 • Audrius Tomonis/www.banknotes.com: 135

ACKNOWLEDGMENTS
Thanks to Gordon N. Bardos, Assistant Director, Harriman Institute, Columbia University,
for his expert reading of this manuscript.

PRECEDING PAGE
Albanian boys in the country's national costume.

Marshall Cavendish Benchmark
99 White Plains Road
Tarrytown, NY 10591
Website: www.marshallcavendish.us

© Marshall Cavendish International (Asia) Private Limited 2005
® "Cultures of the World" is a registered trademark of Marshall Cavendish Corporation.

Series concept and design by Times Editions
An imprint of Marshall Cavendish International (Asia) Private Limited
A member of Times Publishing Limited

Library of Congress Cataloging-in-Publication Data
Knowlton, MaryLee, 1946-
  Albania / by Mary Lee Knowlton.
     p. cm. — (Cultures of the world)
  Includes bibliographical references and index.
  ISBN 0-7614-1852-0
  1. Albania—Juvenile literature. I. Title. II. Series.
  DR910.K6 2005
  949.65—dc22   2004022236

Printed in China

7 6 5 4 3 2 1

CONTENTS

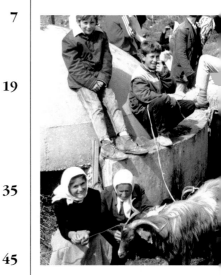

Albanians gather at an animal market.

A traditional Albanian house in the town of Shkodra.

INTRODUCTION

ALBANIA IS A TINY COUNTRY with a history and geography that place it within many of history's biggest stories. Until the 20th century, it had never had a national government of its own, having been dominated by a series of empires—Roman, Greek, Byzantine, and Ottoman, to name just the largest. Through all these subjugations, including the most recent under communism, the Albanian people have maintained their identity, both within and outside of the country's borders.

Today, Albania is an emerging democracy struggling to adjust to a world its people were shut off from for over 50 years. With more Albanians now living outside the country than within and Balkan warfare raging all around, Albania faces many challenges—economic, social, and governmental. In this volume of *Cultures of the World*, we look at the richness of Albania's past, the complexity of its present, and the promise of its future.

GEOGRAPHY

ALBANIA IS A SMALL COUNTRY—11,096 square miles (27,748 square km)—about the size of the state of Maryland. It is located on the southeastern coast of the Adriatic Sea, just across from the heel of the boot of Italy. Its position on the western end of the Balkan Peninsula is of great political significance, and in geographical terms, it makes it a Mediterranean country with distinct seasons and a rich variety of plants and animals.

Albania borders Greece to the south, Macedonia to the east, and Serbia and Montenegro to the northeast. The Adriatic Sea and the Ionian Sea form its western and southwestern borders, respectively, a coastline of 225 miles (362 km) of sunny, sandy beaches.

Albania's land area is made up mostly of hills and mountains, many of them covered with forests. Golem Korab is the highest mountain at 9,032 feet (2,753 m). Coastal plain accounts for about 20 percent of the land.

Left: **Prespa Lake straddles the borders of three countries: Albania, Macedonia, and Greece.**

Opposite: **Albania's landscape consists of hills and mountains. In the valleys, rural Albanians carve out a life for themselves in agriculture.**

The Southern Mountain Region consists of mountains, slopes, gorges, valleys, and streams.

GEOGRAPHICAL REGIONS

Albania has five main geographical regions. The Western Lowlands area along the coastline has a richly varied landscape, from sandy beaches to inland rivers and lakes surrounded by rich farmland. Shkodra Lake (Lake Scutari) in the Northern Lowlands is bordered by a long, lovely beach called the Shiroka. The Adriatic coastline has many bays with clear water and fine sand. The Albanian government sees this area as suitable for development, but the area awaits investors and developers before the tourists are likely to come. The other three geographical regions are all mountainous. The Central Mountain Region lies in the eastern and southeastern part of the country. Golem Korab is located in this region.

The Southern Mountain Region consists of mountain ranges, slopes, and individual mountains. Gorges, mountain streams, and valleys weave their way through the mountain ranges, making this an area of great variety and beauty. The coastal area of this region is known as the Albanian Riviera. The coastal mountains run from Vlona Bay and Drashovica Pass in the north to the Delvina basin in the south, rising dramatically from Vlona Bay to the Mount of Cika, 6,710 feet (2,045 m), then plunging to the Delvina basin.

The Northern Mountain Region is characterized by its cold climate and rich vegetation. The Alps of Albania resemble a big cupola, with pyramid-shaped peaks such as Jezerca at 8,839 feet (2,694 m) and deep valleys, numerous rivers, and glacial lakes. The abundant snowfall and steep slopes would be ideal for skiing, but like the coast, the area awaits development and a sense of stability.

CLIMATE

Albania's climate is classified as mild temperate, with cool, wet winters. Its average low temperature in January, its coldest month, is 41°F (5°C). Its summers are hot and dry, with an average July temperature of 77°F (25°C).

LAKES AND MAIN RIVERS

In the northwestern part of the country is Shkodra Lake (Lake Scutari), the largest lake on the Balkan Peninsula. It covers 142 square miles (368 sq km), with half of its waters in Albania. In the northeast Lake Fierza is named after the hydropower plant that has been built there. Near Lura, 5,248 feet (1,600 m) above sea level, several glacial lakes form a group in the mountains providing a spectacular scenic view.

The main rivers running through Albania are Drini, 177 miles (285 km); Semani, 175 miles (281 km); Vjosa, 169 miles (272 km); Shkumbin, 113 miles (182 km); Mat, 71 miles (115 km); Buna, 27 miles (44 km); Ishm, and Erzen. Only the Buna is navigable.

This small lake is found near Saranda, a town that lies on the Ionian coast in southwestern Albania.

Dandelions, red poppies, and blue wildflowers grow near Prespa Lake.

FLORA

Much of Albania's flora is evergreen, from Mediterranean scrub and flowering plants along the coastal lowlands to Alpine firs in the Northern Mountain Region. More than 3,200 kinds of plants grow in Albania, and over a third of the land is forested.

The coastal strip is covered with maquis, a typical Mediterranean scrub bush. In the north, the coastal plain is cultivated farmland. The southern coastal plain is much hillier and has been terraced with citrus and olive groves. Deciduous forests, mostly beech and oak, cover higher elevations. Just below the tree line at about 6,562 feet (2,000 m) grow forests of birch, pine, and fir. Above them the landscape consists of mountain pastures.

Herbal medicine has a long history in Albania, and it is still practiced in the cities as well as in the villages and rural areas. Every city and town has a marketplace where people can buy the plants or prepared medicines they need. In the countryside, people sometimes sell them at the roadside. Some of the plants widely available include Saint-John's-wort, wild chamomile, lungwort, heartsease, horse-chestnut seed, rue, and thorn apple. Many of these herbs are poisonous when taken in certain amounts or under certain circumstances, but the long, unbroken tradition of use keeps Albanians from making mistakes with them.

FAUNA

Albania's geographical location is responsible for its richly diverse animal population. It is located on the migration route of many birds. More than 350 types of birds are at home in Albania, including grouse, woodcocks, snipes, and pelicans. Land animals include carnivorous brown bears, wolves, foxes, jackals, lynx, and wildcats. Herbivores include wild goats, deer, and hares. Freshwater fish thrive in the lakes and rivers. The most common are sardine, mullet, red mullet, carp, and speckled trout.

The lynx can be found in the wilds of Albania.

Skenderbeg Square in the city of Tirana.

TIRANA

Tirana is the capital city of Albania, founded as a settlement early in the 17th century by Ottoman Turks. Although not much more than a village as late as 1920, it was chosen as the capital primarily because of its central location. When the Italians exerted their influence over the city, they brought their sense of style with them, expanding the city center and building wide boulevards and substantial, elegant ministry buildings, hotels, and palaces. The Communists continued construction during their rule, and today their slogans can still be seen built into the brickwork of some of the buildings.

Tirana is a city of 350,000 people and the political and cultural center of the country. Tirana is introducing modernity to Albania with its Internet cafés and appalling traffic. Young people from all over Albania move there, drawn to its increasingly lively nightlife, though the high rate of unemployment makes their stay tenuous.

Mother Teresa Airport, outside of Tirana, is Albania's only commercial airport. Railroads provide connections to other cities; but Albanians know not to use them, because they are very old and slow, though cheap.

DURRES

Durres, the second largest city in Albania, lies on the Adriatic Sea. It is in a fertile region in which corn, grain, sugar beets, and tobacco are grown and livestock is raised. An important commercial and communications center serving central Albania, the city has a power plant, a dockyard, and factories producing bricks, cigarettes, leather products, and soap. Exports include grain, hides, minerals, and tobacco. The city is linked by rail with Tirana and Elbasan.

Durres is the seat of a Greek Orthodox metropolitan, the primary church official in the province, and, since the fifth century, of a Roman Catholic archbishop. Outside the city are remains of Byzantine and Venetian fortifications.

SHKODRA

Shkodra was founded around the fourth century B.C. and is one of Albania's oldest cities. In the far north of the country, it grew up in the hills surrounding Shkodra Lake where three rivers meet. Initially Shkodra was a tribal center and grew into a capital of the Illyrian kingdom. Over the next thousand years it was an important military and trade route, a Serbian center, and a Venetian possession.

During the 300 years that followed, it resisted and then fell to the Ottoman Turks, finally becoming the economic center of northern Albania, producing silk, tobacco, arms, and silver. During those years Shkodrans built the stone houses that came to be thought of as typically Albanian: two-story houses with shops or stables on the ground floor and living quarters above. They also built an arched bridge, Mesi, that still stands.

By the 18th century Shkodra was also the center of Turkish influence and administration. A lively bazaar was the center of city life. Throughout the 19th century there were many uprisings against the Turks, but Ottoman rule held firm. At the same time, by mid-century there were more than 3,500 shops in Shkodra, and it was an important center of trade for the entire Balkan Peninsula, with a trade administration, a trade court, and an international postage system.

Shkodra was active in the fight for Albanian independence and struggled mightily against attempts of countries like Montenegro, Serbia, and ultimately Yugoslavia to claim it. Shkodrans fought against the Italians

Part of the wall that still stands at the Castle of Rozafa.

in World War II and were in the forefront of the battle against the Communists in 1990 and 1991, in demonstrations and riots fighting against the police.

Today, with a population of 81,000 people, Shkodra is back where it started, an important cultural and economic center of trade. It has flourishing electronics, food processing, and building materials industries. Other industries include wood and leather processing, textiles and clothing, and tobacco.

As a cultural center, Shkodra is home to the Pedagogical Institute, a branch of the University of Tirana; a large library; theater and dance groups; and many museums.

Two very different architectural styles exist in Shkodra. One is old, with narrow streets bordered by high stone walls with gates at each end. But the main part of the city was rebuilt after World War II in the communist-era style of straight, wide streets with blocks of residential and public buildings. A large industrial park has grown up north of the city.

Shkodra has over 90 cultural monuments, many Turkish, such as the Turkish Bath and the Mosque of Plumbi. But the most important is the Castle of Rozafa, which is over 2,400 years old and has a legend associated with it. Rozafa was the bride of the youngest of three brothers. The brothers were told that in order for their castle to stand, someone should be sacrificed. So shortly after the birth of her baby, Rozafa was locked within the walls of the castle. A hole was left in the wall just big enough for her to feed her baby through. People believe that the waters that fall from the stones at the entrance to the castle represent the milk that flowed from her breast.

Lake Shkodra, the largest lake in Albania and in the Balkans, lies on the border between Albania and Serbia and Montenegro. The lake is home to a wide range of fish species.

OTHER CITIES

Butrint, Elbasan, Vlona, and Korce are other important Albanian cities. During the communist years they were centers of manufacturing, but during the unrest following the communist collapse in 1992 and the economic collapse in 1995, many of the factories were damaged or destroyed, and few have reopened. Still, the cities have enormous historical, religious, and cultural meaning for the people and are home to families stretching back through centuries. Butrint, for example, contains the ruins of Roman and Greek civilizations. A World Heritage site, it has many of the features that people travel to Greece and Italy to see, such as a coliseum, a lion's gate, and a Greek temple where the ancients came to partake of the healing waters. It was also a center of Christianity.

ALBANIAN ROADS

Geographically, the experience of driving is influenced by Albania's mountainous terrain, which has limited the creation and maintenance of roads. Since the mid-1990s the roads in the cities have improved remarkably. A coherent system of traffic laws and signs, not to mention driver's instruction, are still needed. Outside of the cities on the mountain roads, driving is a hazardous endeavor. The roads are narrow, twisting, and poorly maintained. Potholes are big enough to pitch an unwary motorist down the unguarded mountainside. Cars and minibuses share the roads with pedestrians and animals. Visitors are advised to travel only during the day, and Albanians don't need to be told.

Still, the views from the mountain roads are astonishingly beautiful, and along the coastline they are as lovely as any in Europe.

The experience of driving in Albania owes much to Albanian history and geography. Historically, the experience is shaped by the fact that until 1991 it was illegal for ordinary Albanians to even own a car, much less drive it. High government functionaries had official cars, however, and their choice of vehicle was the Mercedes-Benz. Though the proletariat was not driving or, in most cases, even riding in cars, they were noticing, and today the Mercedes-Benz is the most frequently seen car on the road. Though the person driving the car probably paid for it, searching of its provenance will more often than not lead to someone in Germany whose car was stolen.

THE HUMAN HISTORY OF ALBANIA begins in the Paleolithic period, roughly 100,000 to 10,000 B.C. Tools retrieved from along the Ionian Sea show that an ancient civilization existed at the foot of Mount Dajti near Tirana.

More recently, around 5000 B.C., a settlement in the southern coastal area left the remains of huts, earthenware, and tools. The civilization known as the Cakran settlement also left vases decorated with painted motifs of human beings. These people were the ancient Illyrians, a loosely formed group of Mediterranean tribes who were ancestors to the peoples of classical Rome and Greece.

From its beginnings, the written history of Albania is a story of hundreds of years of invasions and emigrations. In the third century B.C., an Illyrian tribe, the Ardiacans, established itself at Shkodra, a city in the northern mountains of today's Albania. The Illyrians were known not only as brave and skilled warriors but also as socially evolved and hospitable people. Men and women were of near equal status in the community, with women serving as heads of tribal federations. Illyrians believed in an afterlife. They buried weapons and personal items with the dead for use in the next world. The land was rich in iron, copper, gold, and silver, and Illyrians were skilled miners and metalsmiths. They were also accomplished shipbuilders and sailors. One of their designs became the prototype for the Roman *liburna*, an especially fleet and light warship.

The archeological remains at Butrint (above), with its mosaic floor (opposite), contain evidence of the various cultures—Trojan, Illyrian, and Roman—that have occupied Albania.

Above: **The ruins of Quintum Station date as far back as** A.D. **80.**

Opposite: **The double-headed eagle symbolizes Albania, the "Land of the Eagles." The motif is carved into this wall at the Skenderbeg Museum in Kruja.**

ALBANIA UNDER THE ROMANS

Rome recognized the Illyrian territories as valuable to their designs on lands east of the Adriatic. In 229 B.C. they began their assault on Illyrian lands, and by 168 B.C. Illyria was part of the Roman Empire.

For the next six centuries Rome ruled Illyrian lands. Roman culture and language had a great influence on Illyrian culture, especially in what is now southern Albania. Through the Romans, Christianity came into the culture, where it competed with Illyrian pagan beliefs and cults from the East. As the Roman Empire declined, people of Illyrian descent grew in influence and power especially in the military.

In A.D. 95 the Roman Empire separated into two parts, east and west, and Albania became part of the Byzantine, Eastern, Empire. The first 70 years of Byzantine rule brought raiders from the north, Visigoths, Huns, and Ostrogoths. Then came the Slavs. Though most of the Balkans buckled culturally as well as militarily in the face of the invaders, the Illyrians of modern-day Albania resisted assimilation, maintaining their language and many of their ways. Sometime between the sixth and eighth centuries, the name Illyria gave way to Albanoi, the name of an Illyrian tribe located in what is today central Albania. The name spread from central Albania and was taken up by people throughout the land. Christianity was well entrenched and centered in Rome despite Byzantine rule. For the next several centuries church allegiance would shift repeatedly until northern Albania settled in with Rome and the south with Constantinople.

HOW ALBANIA GOT ITS NAME: A LEGEND

One day a young boy was hunting in the mountains. High above him an eagle flew, carrying a snake in its beak. As the boy watched, the eagle soared even higher, disappearing into a hollow place near the mountaintop. When he saw the eagle fly away, the boy climbed to the place where he had last seen it.

There he found the eagle's nest, and in it a young eaglet playing with the snake. The boy watched in horror as the seemingly dead snake stirred, turning on the young bird. It pulled back its head preparing to pierce the baby bird with its poisonous fangs. With the speed of a great hunter, the boy drew back his bow and killed the snake before it could strike.

Carefully he took the bird from its nest and started back home. Suddenly from above the boy heard a great clamor. The eagle had returned and was circling around his head in great agitation. "Why are you taking my child?" it cried.

"I rescued your child from the snake you failed to kill," said the boy. "Now this child is mine."

"If you return the child to me, I will bestow on you the keenness of my eyes and the power of my wings. You will be invincible in battle. And you shall be known by my name."

The boy returned the baby eagle to be raised by its own. But as they both grew, the eaglet would appear whenever the boy hunted. When he became a man, he was a great hunter and warrior, always guided and protected by the eagle whose life he had saved.

The people of his country grew to love and admire the great hunter and warrior and chose him to be their king. They called him "Albanian," which means son of the eagle, and his kingdom became known as Albania, the land of the eagles.

This Byzantine church in Berat was fitted with many features of Ottoman architecture when the Turks ruled over Albania.

BYZANTINE RULE

The late Middle Ages marked the height of Albanian urban culture. International trade flourished between Albanian cities and the European cities of Venice, Ragusa (today's Dubrovnik), and Thessalonica, now Thessaloniki. The cities's prosperity stimulated growth in education, art, and literature. But significantly, Greek and Latin, not Albanian, were the languages used in cultural and government circles.

Likewise, the Byzantine system of government broke down tribal loyalties and strengths. The land was divided into themes, or military territories. Young men were conscripted for service by their military landlords and returned home to work the land as serfs. An aristocracy formed, especially in the south, rivaling the kinship loyalties of the Illyrian tribes.

Byzantine rule lasted nearly 1,000 years in Albania, but by the end of the 14th century—following raids and rule by Bulgarians, Norman crusaders, Italians, Venetians, and finally, Serbs—thousands of Albanians had emigrated and the country was ripe for picking by the Turks. Whereas the Romans had traveled through Albania as a route to the East, Turkey saw it as a stepping-stone to the West.

SKENDERBEG AND THE RESISTANCE

The Ottoman Turkish invasion began in 1388. By 1430 the Turks controlled the whole country. Then came the resistance that has shaped Albanian pride and identity, a 25-year standoff led by George Kastrioti, known to Albanians then and until this day as Skenderbeg. Born Albanian in 1405, George Kastrioti was conscripted into the Turkish army, where he gained notoriety as a military genius. In 1443 he deserted the Turks and came home

A statue of the national hero, Skenderbeg, who unified the various Albanian princes and led the initial resistance against the Turks.

as Skenderbeg, to unify and lead the Albanian princes in driving out the invaders. For 25 years, from his boyhood home of Kruja, Skenderbeg held off the Turks, providing the only real resistance the Ottoman Empire met in its sweep through the Balkans. It was a hopelessly unequal fight, and its 25-year duration won Skenderbeg and his Albanians the admiration of Europeans.

Skenderbeg's success was stunning; but after his death in 1468, the unity he had inspired among the Albanians collapsed, and with it the organized resistance. By 1506 the Turks were in complete control of the country, and would remain so for the next 400 years.

The Renaissance that would enlighten and shape the rest of Europe was just beginning when the Turks took control of Albania. This was the first stage of Albania's withdrawal from the face of Europe, as it was cut off from the exchange of ideas that shaped Europe's humanistic future.

The Turks had a number of frontier posts which they had to defend from attack during the various Albanian revolts.

TURKISH RULE

Turkish rule was harsh. To escape persecution, one-fourth of the Albanian population fled to southern Italy, Sicily, and the Dalmatian coast. Yet the Turks were never able to fully crush the Albanian spirit. Especially in the northern highlands, they ruled in name only. Tribal authority and loyalty governed the highlanders, and they did not pay taxes, serve in the army, or turn in their arms. Their uprisings were frequent and fierce.

In response to Albanian intransigence, and believing it religiously motivated, the Turks embarked on a program of enforced conversion to Islam. By the end of the 17th century, two-thirds of the Albanian people had become Muslims, many to avoid the enormous taxes levied on Christians. Christianity itself had resulted in religious fragmentation of the population between Rome and Constantinople, and the forced conversions to Islam further politicized the notion of religion. Hundreds of years later, Albanian nationalists would proclaim, "The religion of Albania is Albanianism," in an effort to promote unity.

The Turks ruled Albania under a feudal system that awarded land to military lords who them served well. As the Ottoman Empire began to lose its hold, these lords assumed more autonomy from Constantinople. They became known as pashas, and for several generations two families established separate states in northern Albania and southern Albania and Greece, ruling until the 19th century, when they were overthrown by Turkey.

The rule of the pashas now fell to private landowners, known as beys, in the south and to tribal chieftains in the northern highlands. Peasants in the south worked as tenant farmers for the beys. Albanians in the north lived in patriarchal societies in which the rule of the blood feud established order and expectations for generations.

Once again, many Albanians left the country to advance themselves. Many, however, stayed within the Ottoman Empire and attained high positions in government and the military.

In the 19th century the Turks were beginning to lose their grip on the Balkan countries. In 1878 Albanians living in several Balkan countries met in Kosovo and formed the Prizren League. Their first goal, which would be unsuccessful, was to unite Albanians throughout the Balkans into an autonomous Albanian entity.

The main square in the town of Shkodra, as it was in the early 1900s.

Their second goal was more successful, though it would take nearly 50 years to realize: it was to restore the Albanian language in order to unite Albanians from several countries into one identity. The League became a powerful symbol to Albanians for their national aspirations even though it was suppressed by the Turks for its politics. In 1908 the League met again to adopt a national language and alphabet, which replaced several variations. The national movement now represented the feelings of most Albanians, and when the Turks in 1908 reneged on promises for democratic reform, the Albanians took up arms. After three years of battle, from 1910 to 1912, Albania declared its independence on November 28, 1912.

THE GREAT POWERS

In December 1912 a group of ambassadors from Britain, Germany, Russia, Austria-Hungary, France, and Italy, known as the Great Powers, met in London to deal with issues raised by Albanian independence. Though they recognized the independence of Albania, and thus its right to exist as a separate state, they ignored the ethnic realities of the region. Instead of uniting the Albanians of Albania, Greece, and Kosovo, they ceded Kosovo to Serbia and the southern lands to Greece. This left half of the Albanian people inhabiting the Balkans outside the borders of the new state. While excluding Albanians, the Great Powers included 35,000 Greeks within Albanian's borders. To this day, Kosovo and the Greek population of Albania are troublesome issues.

WORLD WAR I

The Great Powers also appointed a German prince to rule Albania, but he was woefully unprepared. Within six months of his appointment World War I had broken out,

Woodrow Wilson was the 28th president of the United States, holding office from 1913 to 1921. His lone voice saved Albania from being split up by the Great Powers among its neighboring countries.

and he gladly went home. As part of the war effort, the armies of Austria-Hungary, France, Italy, Greece, Montenegro, and Serbia invaded and occupied Albania, which by this time had assumed its present size, approximately that of the state of Maryland. By the time the war ended, Albania was in chaos, without leaders or a real government. At the Paris Peace Conference after the war, Britain, France, and Italy proposed to partition Albania among its bordering countries. Only the veto of President

Woodrow Wilson of the United States salvaged the tiny country. (Streets all over Albania are named after Woodrow Wilson.) In 1920 an Albanian national congress formed a new government. In December of that year, Albania—this time with the help of Britain—was admitted to the League of Nations and was recognized for the first time as a sovereign nation.

Now Albania's challenge was to reconcile two very different groups. One was composed of conservative landowners from the Ottoman past, led by a chieftain from the north-central part of the country, Ahmed Bey Zogu. The other group was led by Fan S. Noli, a bishop of the Orthodox Church who had been educated in the United States. His group was largely liberal and pro-democratic, consisting mainly of politicians, merchants, and intellectuals who were relying on the West and on their Albanian communities there to modernize their country and lead them into the 20th century. Neither leader could bridge the gap caused by competing factions and goals.

Still, the liberal forces gathered strength and unified their appeal. In 1924 there was a successful peasant revolt and Zogu sought refuge in Yugoslavia. Noli became prime minister and set out to build a Western-style democracy in Albania, embarking on a program of land reform. But he was slow in carrying out his program, his treasury was depleted, and his government was too far left to gain international support. After just six months he was overthrown in a revolt led by the returning Zogu.

Ahmed Bey Zogu was forced out of Albania in 1924. A year later, he overthrew Fan S. Noli with the help of the Russians he had be-friended in Yugoslavia.

King Zog and the royal family in traditional Albanian attire.

KING ZOG

Zogu thus began a 14-year reign in Albania—first as president (1925–28), then as King Zog I (1928–39). The social base of Zog's power was a coalition of southern beys, landowners, and northern *bajraktars* (bah-YRAH-ktahrs), tribal leaders. With the support of his coalition, an efficient police force, and Italian financing, King Zog brought stability to Albania. Under his rule the tribes of the highlands acknowledged the central government's authority. The rampant lawlessness that had characterized the country was curbed. The society of the cities began to show some similarity to the social life of Western countries, and he initiated universal education, at least in concept.

However, his rule was characterized by failure because he did not carry out a policy of land reform. The people of Albania were left as impoverished in independence as they had been as a Turkish colony. Moreover, though his country was formally a constitutional monarchy, it was actually just a dictatorship. As had happened so often before, thousands of Albanians migrated to other countries where life held a brighter promise. Those who remained grew increasingly disillusioned as Zog continued to thwart democratic rule. Eventually Zog's rule alienated most of the intellectual class and caused unrest among the working classes. His refusal to accommodate democracy and his failure to make the economy work led to the formation of communist groups in Albania.

The country was unstable both politically and socially. Zog signed several accords with Italy to bring financial relief to Albania, but they had only a short-term effect and did not expand the economy, especially since the world was by now in the midst of the Great Depression. On the very tenuous basis of these accords, in 1939 the Fascist government of Italy invaded and occupied the country. King Zog fled once again, this time to Greece.

Albania's minister of foreign affairs, Gemmi Dino (with pen in hand), signs the Italo-Albanian Diplomatic Pact.

WORLD WAR II

In the meantime, World War II had broken out. Italy's occupation of Albania gave it a base for invading Greece, but the Greeks rebuffed the attack and the Italians withdrew back into Albania. The Germans were more successful in Greece and Yugoslavia, and reunited the Albanian regions of Greece and Kosovo with Albania once again. They also replaced the Italians as the occupying force in Albania. On the verge of losing the war, Germany withdrew from Albania. In November 1944, Kosovo was returned to Yugoslavia, and Cameria, the Greek part of Albania, reverted to Greece.

Throughout World War II the Albanian resistance was fiercely active against the Italian and the German occupiers. The resistance was largely composed of members of the communist groups that had formed in opposition to King Zog, and now these groups became one party, the Albanian Communist Party, under the leadership of Enver Hoxha. On November 29, 1944, the Communists seized control of the government. As secretary-general of his party, Enver Hoxha became prime minister. In 1946 the country renamed itself the People's Republic of Albania.

Enver Hoxha giving an impassioned speech during a rally in 1945.

PEOPLE'S REPUBLIC

When World War II ended, the Albanian government feared that Yugoslavia, which had helped install the Albanian Communist Party, was moving to annex or otherwise assume power in Albania. Once again faced with loss of autonomy, the government established the form of control that would

HOXHA

For nearly 50 years the government and life in Albania was defined and controlled by Enver Hoxha. Born in 1908, Hoxha distinguished himself in World War II as a leader of the resistance against the Italian occupation and a founder of Albania's Communist Party. Nationalistic to the point of paranoia, he increasingly isolated his country, first from the Western countries, and in the end from former allies China and the Soviet Union. In his lifetime Hoxha held the positions of general secretary of the Albanian Communist Party, premier of Albania, minister of foreign affairs, and commander and chief of the army, sometimes all at one time. Hoxha's brand of communism was a fervent devotion to the Marxist-Stalinist ideal of centralized power in both government and economy. The population of postwar Albania was made up of subsistence farmers—80 percent of whom were illiterate—living without electricity or plumbing, and with a life expectancy of 40 years. Hoxha brought education and industry to the country by creating schools, relocating workers to factories, and collectivizing farms. Executions and imprisonment eliminated all opposition, actual, potential, and imaginary.

Ill health in the last 10 years of his life kept Hoxha from day-to-day rule, but his authority was so well established that his subordinates carried on his ideas in his name and no other ruler took his place. He spent these later years writing theory and memoirs that articulated the positions that increasingly isolated him and his country from the rest of the world, a belief in the absolute power of the state. When he died in 1985, many Albanians cried for fear that they would be arrested if they did not. By then, the literacy rate was nearly 100 percent and life expectancy had increased to over 70 years. At the same time, Albania was the poorest and least developed country in Europe.

persist for the next 50 years, a Soviet-style political dictatorship. While Stalin lived, Albania and the Soviet Union were mutually supportive. But when Stalin died, the Albanian government lost faith in the Soviet Union's ability to safeguard Albania's independence. Though the Soviet Union remained staunchly communist, during the late 1950s it rejected some of the excesses of Stalinism. The other countries in Eastern Europe began to exhibit a diversity that was alarming to Albania's more conservative government, still fiercely devoted to Stalinist policies.

To solidify its power, the Hoxha government conducted purges of the moderates within the party. Thousands were executed or imprisoned. A campaign to minimize foreign influence further isolated Albania from the outside world. The government moved people living in the cities to the countryside to work on collective farms in order to discourage the association of intellectuals and activists.

A POLICE STATE

Albania was now a police state. Strict obedience and conformity were expected and enforced. All dissent was repressed. Religion was illegal, and Albania proclaimed itself the first officially atheist nation. Travel was severely limited within, and forbidden outside, the country. It was illegal to own a car. Even naming babies was regulated. Parents consulted a list of acceptable names that changed each year. Sometimes the names were made up, like Marenglen, which is composed of the first three letters of Marx, Engels, and Lenin. Wives of disgraced party members were forced to divorce their husbands. Complaining about food shortages was cause for family imprisonment.

A secret police force, called the Sigurimi, monitored all human activity. Neighbors and even family members became informers and spies, with children trained to spy on parents. Punishable crimes included listening to banned radio programs or expressing disrespect for Enver Hoxha. If one person was found in violation of the law, the whole family, parents and grandparents as well, could be sent to a prison camp, where they would be tortured and sometimes allowed to starve to death.

Today the National Historical Museum lists the toll of Hoxha's reign as 17,900 imprisoned, 5,157 killed, and 30,383 exiled. Many Albanians think these numbers woefully understate the reality, which they believe was that hundreds of thousands of people disappeared into the prison camp system, where they were killed or worked to death.

ISOLATION

As its relations with the Soviet Union faltered, Albania forged ties with China, both out of admiration for China's similar cultural revolution and a recognition that the two countries were so far apart that China couldn't possibly invade. Until about 1976 China provided some economic assistance to Albania, but that ended when Mao Tse-tung died. For the next 15 years Albania had virtually no allies or partners. Its people were so isolated and deluded that some thought they were living in the most prosperous and advanced country in Europe.

During these years the Albanian economy declined. A lack of trading partners meant that whatever Albania could not produce could not be had. Machinery and technology wore out and became outdated. As a result, industrial and agricultural productivity declined, though the demands made on workers kept production levels higher than they might otherwise have been. Although the early years of industrialization had led to advances over the prewar years in the supply of electricity and infrastructure, the systems deteriorated as the economy failed to support them.

After Hoxha's death in 1985, the country was run by Ramiz Alia with little change in policy. Alia continued the pattern of isolation from both East and West. Domestically, he preserved inherited policies of religious persecution and political oppression.

Ramiz Alia's rise to power within the Albanian Communist Party was largely due to the influence of Enver Hoxha.

WINDS OF CHANGE

In the late 1980s change was in the wind throughout Eastern Europe and the Soviet Union. The flow of information had become somewhat harder to control as radio stations from neighboring countries broadcast news of change and development in the region. The median age of

These busts of Joseph Stalin (left) and Enver Hoxha were found in a warehouse where they had been abandoned when communist rule ended in Albania.

Albanians was just 25, and the young were cautiously looking for improvement. Perhaps most significantly, the limitations of a centrally controlled, underdeveloped agrarian economy were becoming unavoidably clear: with the youthful population growing, the economy simply could not absorb them. Shortages of energy and imported materials prevented the industrial sector from expanding though demand for industrial products remained high.

The government began to promote some changes. It instituted policies of worker incentives, rewarding productivity. It allowed limited criticism of bureaucratic planning and policies, though it was disinclined to make any changes based on such criticism, and workers were similarly disinclined to criticize. Workers who had seen nothing good come from overachieving or from critical thinking in the past met these tiny steps of change with skepticism and fear. They did not believe that change could come from within the system.

By 1989 communism had all but collapsed throughout Eastern Europe, and the Albanian people became more restive. Intellectuals, the working class, and the young began to agitate against the communist government. Alia lifted restrictions. He allowed people to travel abroad, permitted the free practice of religion, and adopted an open-market policy for the economy.

Finally, in December 1990 he allowed the creation of independent political parties. This was the end of the Communist monopoly of power. In 1992 Albanians elected a non-communist government, and Alia resigned as president. His replacement was Sali Berisha, head of the Democratic Party. Albania's international isolation was officially ended.

Sali Berisha was elected head of state in Albania's first general elections after the fall of communism.

Albania's efforts to establish a free-market economy proceeded at an unsteady pace, but its progress brought international financial aid. In the following years, governments would rise and fall amidst scandal and corruption. In 1997 Albania suffered a breakdown of nearly all social order when its economy collapsed. During the previous year the corrupt government had urged the citizens to invest their savings in what turned out to be a pyramid scheme. Nearly half of the citizens invested their life savings, a total of about two billion dollars. When, inevitably, the scheme collapsed, the entire government and the citizenry were left bankrupt. Thousands of people rioted for months, destroying infrastructure the country could ill afford to lose or replace. Mobs raided military arms stores and weapons depots and stole thousands of weapons—Kalashnikovs, mines, and bombs. At least 1,500 people were killed.

GOVERNMENT

THE OFFICIAL NAME of Albania is Republika e Shqiperise, "Land of Eagles," but to Albanians it is Shqiperia. Albania is considered to be an emerging democracy. As such, it operates under a constitution ratified in 1998, with a government chosen in free elections. However, though its laws and constitution are codified, it is necessary to recognize the enormity of the challenge the people and their government face as they emerge from the tyranny and isolation that determined their lives for centuries.

Opposite: **An Albanian girl helps her father deposit a voting slip during elections in July 2001.**

ALBANIAN FLAG AND NATIONAL ANTHEM

The Albanian flag is a black, two-headed eagle on a red background adopted in 1992. Its significance goes back to Skenderbeg. After abandoning the Turkish army, he returned to his father's home in Kruja. Above the castle he flew a red flag with the double eagle, his family seal, as a symbol of his return. With the castle and the flag behind him he proclaimed: "I have not brought you liberty. I found it among you." The Albanian nobles united behind him and, for the next 25 years, they held off the invading Turks. In modern times, the flag has variously borne a helmet, a hammer and sickle, and finally a star. After the fall of communism the star was removed and the flag returned to its original design.

The Albanian national anthem was written as a poem, published first in 1912. The poet called himself Asdreni, a combination of sounds from his full name Aleks Stavra Drenova. When he first published his poem he called it *Pledge to the Flag*, but later he renamed it *Dreams and Tears*. It was set to the music of Romanian composer Ciprian Porumbescu.

United around the flag,
With one desire and one goal,
Let us pledge our word of honor
To fight for our salvation.
Only he who is a born traitor
Averts from the struggle.
He who is brave is not daunted,
But falls—a martyr to the cause.

With arms in hand we shall remain,
To guard our fatherland round about.
Our rights we will not bequeath,
Enemies have no place here.
For the Lord Himself has said,
That nations vanish from the earth,
But Albania shall live on,
Because for her, it is for her that we fight.

POLITICS BEFORE 1994

Centuries of Ottoman rule, followed by the authoritarian government of a self-proclaimed king, and then by 50 years of isolation under the most repressive communist government in the world have left Albanians inexperienced in self-government or even free thought. The difficulty of establishing a market economy or attracting foreign investment has led to widespread unemployment, government corruption, organized crime, and general dissatisfaction and mistrust.

It might seem that offered the chance to decide their own destiny in all matters, people who had lived under tyrannical repression would gladly seize the opportunity. But like people in other parts of the world living under tyranny, Albanians had developed priorities that superseded a desire for freedom. Foremost among these was a desire for safety. Albania has become safer in the 21st century than in the last decade of the 20th, but security can still be elusive, and many Albanians are willing to trade a degree of freedom for greater safety.

Though elections are free, the fiercely partisan nature of Albanian politics often results in boycotts of government institutions by one party or another. The police, both secret and civil, are largely unaware of the rights usually accorded to a free people—the rights of free speech, free assembly, and a free press. Opposition to government programs and officials can bring harassment at least, and often more severe reprisals. Government employees have been known to lose their jobs or be inconveniently transferred for expressing negative opinions or even failing to demonstrate sufficient enthusiasm.

A NEW CONSTITUTION

In 1994 Albanians were offered a new constitution to be ratified by referendum. The broadcast media, as clearly state-controlled as they had been under communism, relentlessly promoted its passage. The proposed constitution would have guaranteed Albanians most of the rights and freedoms other European countries had lived with since World War II or earlier. Though the constitution, to all who looked at it, seemed to be what they wanted, the vote represented a chance to show disapproval of the government. The people rejected the constitution.

This young boy takes part in a politcal rally in a run-up to the elections.

The constitution finally passed in 1998, though the opposition Democratic Party boycotted the elections and there were charges of widespread fraud and corrupt voting practices.

The constitution provides for free elections every four years. All people over the age of 18 vote to choose 100 of the 140 legislators of the People's Assembly. The remaining 40 are chosen by the Assembly itself according to the proportions each party wins in the popular election.

The Parliament Building in Tirana.

THE GOVERNMENT

The People's Assembly elects the president. The president of the republic since 2002 is Alfred Moisiu. The president appoints the prime minister, who is the head of the government. The current prime minister is Fatos Nano. The prime minister selects a council of ministers, who are approved by the president.

The judicial system is called the Supreme Court, and the People's Assembly elects its chairman to a four-year term.

Albania has little experience in organizing political parties or developing a cooperative, or even civil, way of working together. Disagreements are strident, and sometimes even violent. Political functionaries of opposing parties are mistrustful of each other at best, and compromise is less common than denunciation.

Albania is divided into 36 districts. Several districts are then grouped into a county, of which there are 12. The county is the main administrative division. The capital city, Tirana, has a special status.

DOMESTIC ISSUES

Many of Albania's domestic problems date from the collapse of the economy and subsequent unrest of 1997. The prisons were either destroyed or damaged, and all the prisoners escaped. Although five prisons have been reopened, only about 300 of the 1,200 inmates are again in custody. Even with many of its convicts at large, the prison system's facilities are still inadequate.

The government has taken steps to improve the treatment of ethnic minorities, always a problem in the Balkan countries. Greek elementary schools are now common in Greek communities, and the Greek language has been legitimized as a school course. Likewise, students can study the Macedonian language in the districts bordering Macedonia. As in many countries, Romany (Gypsies) form the most neglected group. They suffer high illiteracy, poor health conditions, and disadvantages in employment and housing.

The recovery of Albania from the 1997 uprising and economic failures was further complicated by the persecution of ethnic Albanians in Kosovo. By 1998 Albania had taken in 40,000 Kosovar Albanians fleeing for their lives. In the first half of 1999, as the Yugoslav army increased the rate and scale of the atrocities, NATO responded with military actions against Yugoslavia. Eight hundred thousand Albanians fled Kosovo seeking shelter in neighboring countries and beyond. More than 500,000 got no farther than Albania. NATO, the United Nations, and several other organizations erected large refugee camps all over Albania, where the refugees waited until they could return or go elsewhere. This caused serious food shortages. The camps themselves had no sanitation or sewer systems, and waste was dumped, if at all, directly into the water supply. Support from international relief agencies was generous, but the crisis taxed an already unstable government.

Ethnic Albanians from Kosovo make their way into northern Albania.

Albanian prime minister Fatos Nano (left) paid a visit to his Macedonian counterpart Hari Kostov (right) in June 2004.

FOREIGN POLICY

Upward of four million Albanians live outside the country, and this situation shapes much of the country's foreign policy and actions. Albania's relations with its neighbors are often ambivalent. Because ethnic Albanians in other countries look to Albania for support and sometimes protection, Albania tries to maintain diplomatic ties with its neighbors, such as Greece, Italy, Macedonia, and Kosovo. It also seeks the protection of European Union countries and the United States.

Relations between Albania and Macedonia have improved since the two countries signed an economic cooperation agreement in July 1999, promoting cooperation in the fields of energy, mining, and trade. Both countries also plan to build new power lines to link border towns. Albania will supply a metallurgy plant in Tetovo with chrome. The two countries have also agreed to cooperate in improving the environment around Lake Ohrid and Lake Prespa, which are in both countries.

Throughout the 1990s relations with Greece ranged from tense to quite hostile, with tens of thousands of Albanians expelled from Greece. However, in 1999 the two countries launched two joint projects. One is a gas pipeline that will run from Algeria through Italy and Albania to Greece. The other is the construction of a highway along the Adriatic Sea that will link both Greece and Albania with Montenegro and Croatia. These projects will benefit Albania's infrastructure, which is notably primitive. Equally important, they mark the beginning of Albania's interaction with another country as a reliable and stable partner.

Italy has long had an economic and somewhat proprietary interest in Albania, but today its principal interest is in Albanian migrant workers who are settling in southern parts of Italy. The situation became acute in 1997, when thousands of Albanians fled their country for Italy. Italy intervened militarily in Albania to restore the legal government's authority in 1997. During the Kosovo crisis another refugee influx from Kosovo to Italy via Albania was reported. Organized criminal activity has made the smuggling of illegal immigrants, willing and unwilling, a lucrative business. Italy is the first destination, and from there people are shipped throughout Europe.

Relations with the United States and the European Union are relatively good. Albania is considered to be of strategic importance to NATO, and, for its part, wants to be militarily affiliated with it. Albania was the first post-communist country to apply for NATO membership. The request was turned down, but Albania joined the Partnership for Peace program, the first step toward full NATO membership, in February 1994. In 2003 it supported the United States and Britain in the war against Iraq.

In addition to Albania, two other post-communist countries—Croatia ad Macedonia—are seeking full NATO membership. On March 29, 2004, U.S. President George Bush opened the doors of the White House to the prime ministers of these three countries. Standing from left to right are Prime Minister Ivo Sanader of Croatia, Prime Minister Branko Crvenkovski of Macedonia, President George W. Bush of the United States, NATO Secretary General Jaap de Hoop Scheffer, and Prime Minister Fatos Nano of Albania.

ECONOMY

THE COMMUNIST PARTY of Albania came to power in 1941 in a country that had no paved roads, virtually no electricity outside the cities, no industry, and a primitive, subsistence level of farming. Few people could read, and there was no public education.

Over the next 50 years the government—largely in isolation, but with some economic help from the Soviet Union and China—developed cities, built factories, extended the availability of electric power, and organized agriculture into large, government-owned collective farms. Public school policies made education mandatory for boys and girls for the first time in the country's history. Planning and organizing was centrally controlled, with goals and assignments set by the party.

Today, there are still too few paved roads outside the cities. Many of the villages are without electricity. The electricity even in the cities is erratically available, making industry marginally productive and unpredictable. The country has no domestic airlines, so people flying from one city to another within the country have to fly out of the country and then back in. Even then, there is only one commercial airport, so landing in any city but Tirana requires a private plane and a pilot experienced in landing under challenging conditions. Thirty percent of the people live in poverty, and the country has the lowest standard of living in Europe.

Farmers in Lushnja load their baskets with olives (opposite), ready to be taken to the weekly market in Berat (above).

Women in Kruja gather hay on a state-owned farm.

THE ECONOMY BEFORE 1997

Central planning and government ownership were key elements in the communist economy. The good thing about the plan was that everybody shared equally in the wealth. The bad things about the plan were that it did not produce much wealth and people worked very hard or not very hard for the same reward, which was little indeed. Hoxha's iron rule kept people from rebelling against inequities in work requirements or their poverty, and the system itself held firm even though the country did not prosper. The system did not regard hard work or accomplishment as something to be rewarded, and Albanian workers never saw any benefit from exerting themselves. This would come to be a communist legacy that would be hard to supplant when the economic system changed.

When the communist government fell in 1990, it left a population totally without resources or experience in a free market. With the degradation of the infrastructure and lack of money or management skills, the people were left in an economic vacuum of sorts. Gross domestic product (GDP) fell 50 percent from what it had been in 1989. For many there seemed to be only two options: emigration or crime. Many did emigrate, and many still do today. Nearly 20 percent of the country's labor force works abroad, mostly in Greece and Italy. They send back between 300 and 400 million dollars a year, which helps to offset a badly tilted balance of trade.

Organized crime found an easy foothold in a country with few laws and a corrupt or cowed police force. As late as 2002, some police officers stopping cars to check for contraband wore hoods to protect themselves and their families from retaliation by organized crime members. Others hooded themselves to hide their identities so they could act without accountability.

In the early 1990s the government embarked on an enthusiastic program to convert the economic system from centrally organized totalitarian control to a free-market system. To that end they privatized most businesses, industries, and agriculture; encouraged outside investment; and liberalized prices and currency exchange. They also began to establish laws and banking practices that would conform to international expectations.

As the economy moved toward the free-market system, this family was able to set up a small grocery store of their own.

ECONOMIC COLLAPSE

In 1997 the government set up a series of pyramid schemes supposedly aimed at stimulating the economy. They encouraged the populace, fearful of disobeying authority and desperate for money, to invest their savings. They promised enormous returns on the investments. The early investors, mostly government functionaries and others who planned the programs, took their profits from the income generated by later investors. Ultimately and inevitably, the schemes collapsed, and the economy collapsed with them. Early investors fled with their profits or secreted them in foreign accounts, but most of the people of Albania lost everything.

Many Albanians engage in pastoral farming. Livestock such as sheep (below) and cows are a source of meat and dairy products.

The ensuing chaos left Albania resembling a country that had just lost a war. People rioted and destroyed buildings and infrastructure. The rule of law ceased to exist. Foreign aid workers who had supplied many social services were recalled home, and foreign investors lost any interest in Albania as a developing market or producer.

RECOVERY

Since then, the economy has slowly recovered. But it continues to be hampered by poor infrastructure and banking practices. The government has recognized the seriousness of its transportation problems and is working to improve its roads outside and inside the cities. Unfortunately, though it does not show up in official accounting systems, a great deal of Albania's economy is controlled by organized criminal activity in drug and human trafficking. This does not inspire international confidence in its ability to produce goods, make money, and protect investments.

A farmer and his wife in the Drin valley employ the traditional farming method using livestock.

Sixty percent of Albania's workforce is employed in agriculture. Main crops are grains, tobacco, and sugar beets. Livestock is also raised to supply both meat and dairy products. In order to reach its full economic potential, Albania's farm industry will need a large infusion of aid to modernize its equipment. When the farms were privatized in the early 1990s, what existing mechanized equipment they had was outdated and worn-out. Current small landowners cannot afford to replace or maintain this machinery, so much of the farm equipment is now powered by livestock or human effort. Profitability is also affected by the difficulty of getting produce to market over Albania's poor road system.

NATURAL RESOURCES

Albania is rich in mineral resources, especially oil, lignite, copper, chromium, limestone, salt, bauxite, and natural gas. Mining, agricultural processing, and the manufacture of textiles, clothing, lumber, and cement are among the major industries. Chemical, iron, and steel plants were developed under communism, and some of them are still operating, though less productively than before.

Albania has several hydroelectric plants that produce 97 percent of its electricity, but they cannot supply all the electricity the country needs, and the electricity supply is unreliable. The country imports about five times as much electricity as it produces. The shortage of energy has been especially hard on small businesses that operate on very little margin for error. The government currently plans to improve the reliability of the supply of electricity. Increasing hydroelectric power in Albania is difficult at present because funds are not available to create ways to harness it. International investment has not been forthcoming because of Albania's reputation for corruption and financial unreliability. When these problems are effectively addressed, Albania has the resources to produce enough electrical power for its own use and for export to other countries in Europe.

Albania has a wide variety of energy resources ranging from oil and gas, coal, and other fuels, to hydropower, natural forest biomass, and other renewable energy.

TOURISM

The natural beauty of Albania's mountains and its long, sandy beaches offer the promise for the development of all kinds of tourism, and particularly for the development of elite resorts as exist elsewhere in Europe.

There are two main areas with potential for tourism development. Coastal zones, primarily the Adriatic coast from Velipoja to Vlona Bay and the Ionian coast from Llogara to the Greek border, would be ideal for resorts and conference facilities. Interior zones, primarily lake and mountain areas, are suitable for more adventuresome tourists who like to experience the country they are visiting.

The Tirana International Hotel in the capital of Albania plays host to many tourists.

Developing tourism is one of the Albanian government's main economic priorities in the hope that it will account for half of the country's income in the near future. To that end, it is committed to rehabilitating and then maintaining the country's road network, developing and rehabilitating its ports in Durres and Vlona, building new ports, and opening airports that meet acceptable civil air standards to serve more cities than Tirana. Private, probably international, financing will be needed to meet these goals.

INTERNATIONAL AID

Government corruption and instability as well as the daunting presence of organized crime have left foreign governments and international investors unwilling or at least disinclined to contribute on a large scale to the reconstruction of Albania's economy.

Still, foreign aid has come to Albania in many less traditional ways. International relief agencies have set up programs, religious groups have put young people to work, and cities and organizations have sponsored schools and social programs for the relief of targeted populations.

FOREIGN TRADE

Albania's foreign trade goes through the port cities of Durres and Vlona. Exports include agricultural products and mined resources. Albania imports machinery and other manufactured and consumer goods and is a member of both the International Monetary Fund and the World Bank.

Albania's major trade partners are Italy, Greece, Germany, Turkey, Bulgaria, the United States, Austria, Switzerland, United Kingdom, and France. The main export partners are Italy, Greece, Germany, Austria, Macedonia, and Yugoslavia. The main import partners are Italy, Greece, Germany, Turkey, Bulgaria, the United States, Switzerland, and France.

Albania's economic condition is still serious. But it is better than it was, and it is improving. Albania started 1990 as the poorest and most backward country in Europe. It has suffered devastating reverses several times since, but it continues to make progress. The credit goes to Albanians both inside and outside the country who continue to work for a productive and free country.

The port at Durres.

ENVIRONMENT

USUALLY AN ACCOUNT of the condition of the environment of a country pertains to the animals, the plants, and the quality of the water and air in the area. Albania has another, more pressing matter of concern: land mines. Fifty years of communist rule followed by little but chaos and conflict have left Albania with a land mine presence that makes parts of the country uninhabitable by most human standards. It has hindered the development of transportation routes, including railroads and highways. It has enhanced the fears of the people throughout the country, making repatriation of refugees both difficult and dangerous. It has discouraged foreign investment and tourism.

Opposite: **On September 22, 2003, Fatos Nano, the Albanian prime minister, rode a bicycle through the city of Tirana in support of an initiative called "A Day Without Your Car." On that day, no cars were allowed to be driven on the roads of the capital.**

Below: **Signs such as this can be found at Albanian border posts. They advise people on how to recognize land mines.**

MINA

GJITHMONE QENCRONI MBI RRUGE TE
MOS FRKNI DEJECTET E CYSHUARA

Albanian soldiers have been instructed on how to use portable detectors to seek out land mines planted by the Serbs.

LAND MINES

What exactly is a land mine? The Ottawa Convention, convened by the international community to deal with antipersonnel weapons, defines it as "a mine designed to be exploded by the presence, proximity, or contact of a person and that will incapacitate, injure, or kill one or more persons." A land mine is an explosive device placed just under the surface of the land, hidden from view. It explodes when a person or animal steps on it, picks it up, or disturbs the trip wire that is attached to set it off. The land mine explosion can result in amputation, third-degree burns, deep lacerations, broken bones, deafness, blindness, or death. Victims of land mines often suffer from psychological damage resulting from their trauma.

Albania is known to have had over 1.5 million land mines. Many of these mines were set by the Serbs along Albania's northern border during hostilities between Serbia and Kosovo in the late 1990s. However, during its communist years Albania accumulated an enormous stockpile of weapons, stored in over 100 ammunition dumps throughout the country. When the government-sponsored pyramid scheme collapsed in 1997, angry Albanians looted the weapons depots.

Neither the international community nor the resource-deprived Albanian government has been completely successful in ridding Albania of the land mines that contaminate the land. But there has been some progress.

The Partnership for Peace program, sponsored by NATO, worked with the Albanian government, principally the military, to dispose of the

munitions previously stored by the communist government. Many of these weapons are obsolete, but still dangerous. The goals of the project were to assess the number and location of the weapons, remove them to a disposal site, and destroy them. Canada, the partner country, supplied much of the expertise, but it was also an important goal of the project to train the Albanians themselves to do this work efficiently and safely. The mines were destroyed through a process called reverse assembly, which left most of the parts intact. A positive by-product was the recycling of the components of the mines, metal from the containers and ammonite from the explosives.

The project was quite successful, though the enormity of the problem leaves much left to do. Albania has destroyed many of its own accumulated antipersonnel weapons, but those planted along the northern border by the Serbs still remain largely in place because there are no maps telling where they have been set.

These submarines were destroyed during the civil uprising in 1997. In 2002 Albania made a decision to either scrap or sell off much of its antiquated military equipment in an effort to modernize its defense forces.

POLLUTION AND CLEANUP INITIATIVES

Albania is rich in natural resources highly valued by other countries in Europe: expansive forests, fertile soil, and large freshwater supplies. However, these resources were seriously degraded by unregulated industrial activities during its communist years. Between 1944 and 1991 emission controls and wastewater treatment were not incorporated into most factory designs. In the agricultural collectives, where half of Albania's labor force worked, resources were invested in irrigating and fertilizing farmland, but environmental protection and soil conservation were not on the agenda.

In the years since the fall of communism, the demands on the poverty-stricken new democracy left few resources to allocate to the regeneration of the environment. In one regard, the environment actually benefited from the poor economy, as nearly half of the plants and factories closed and their contribution to the pollution of the air, water, and soil ceased. At the same time, the influx of hundreds of thousands of refugees from Kosovo and other Balkan areas placed increased demands on a country where wastewater is released untreated into the sources from which it came.

PARKS AND RESERVES

Albania has a well-defined system of parks and reserves. Four nature reserves are maintained strictly for scientific research; public access is prohibited. But 11 reserves are national parks, protected areas set aside for ecosystem protection as well as recreation. Management itself is minimal, with no maps and few maintained trails, but the scenery is stunning. Hiking, though challenging, offers opportunities to observe migrating birds.

This situation is beginning to change as the economy improves and Albania and the region around it become more stable.

Four sites of dangerous pollution have been identified in Albania. The government is working with international environmental groups to improve conditions and clean up years of damage at the chemical plant in Durres, the fertilizer plant in Vlona, the oil fields in Patos, and the solid-waste dump site in Sharra. Some of these places have been closed, but others remain open and necessary to the Albanian economy and infrastructure. They all require attention, either to improve their present practices or remediate the soil and water problems resulting from years of damage. The risk to human health and the environment is already evident.

Albania will need help from the international community to acquire the technology and money to make the necessary changes. It will also need to work closely with neighboring countries, such as Macedonia. The laws and regulations needed to alleviate, if not necessarily resolve, these environmental problems already exist. But implementing them will require strong leadership. At present the responsibility is divided among agencies and departments whose agendas are in conflict. As the government and economy stabilize and strengthen, so will Albania's environment.

Children's organizations such as the Association of Guides and Scouts have directed their attention to ways they can help improve the environment. A group in Tirana has planted trees, collected garbage, and distributed trash bags in their hometown. Perhaps even more clearly than adults, these children see that these efforts can be made more effectively by civilians than by government agencies.

Opposite: **Daan Everts (left) from the Organization for Security and Cooperation in Europe (OSCE) stops for a word with Albanian prime minister Fatos Nano (right) after both had helped schoolchildren in Tirana collect garbage.**

ALBANIANS

SITUATED AT THE CROSSROADS of Eastern Europe and the West, Albania has for centuries been subject to invasions and occupations. At the very least, it was a patch of land that people from north or south, east or west, felt entitled to pass through on their way somewhere else. When the communist government slammed shut the borders, leaving the land inaccessible to outsiders, some Albanians felt that this was not such a bad idea. As long as they kept their defenses strong, they were no longer at the mercy of other countries.

ALBANIANS IN EXILE

The shutdown of the borders resulted in a strange separation of people who called themselves Albanians from the Albanians then locked inside Albania. The repeated partitioning of Albania by outsiders has resulted in an international situation in which some 3.5 million Albanians live in Albania and perhaps just as many live outside—mostly in Kosovo, Macedonia, Italy, and Greece. Outside of the country, Albanians create strong communities that become "little Albanias." While expatriates, or exiles, tend to look forward to repatriation, Albanians as a rule do not.

During the communist years Albanians were likely to be well educated, so many of those in exile are professionals. Yet in their adopted countries they are often underemployed, and it is not unusual for someone working as a waitress or cleaning woman to be trained in chemistry or engineering. Throughout the other Balkan countries especially, prejudice against and fear of Albanians confines many men to employment as farm laborers or delivery men, jobs that keep them from entering their employers' houses. Underemployed though they are, these emigrants often support several people back in Albania, where unemployment runs high.

The 1990s saw hundreds of thousands of Albanians, mostly young men, leave the country in search of employment, heading for Western Europe and the United States. In the 21st century the flow continues unabated.

Opposite: **Albanian children often have no proper playground so they make use of whatever open ground they can find to play their games.**

61

GHEGS AND TOSKS

Albanians trace their ancestry to the ancient Illyrian tribes that evolved into the Greek and Roman peoples. Over 95 percent of the people in Albania have historically fallen into two groups, one-fifth northern Ghegs and the remainder southern Tosks. In addition, 5 percent of the people come from non-Albanian groups. Though the numbers are in dispute, officially around 2 percent of them are Greek, and the others are Romany, or Gypsy; Serb; and Vlach, or Romanian.

Documents from 14th century travelers refer to a warlike people along the southeastern Adriatic coast who lived in tents that they packed up and moved as they needed to, rather than establish fortified camps. One observer noted that they were superb archers and lancers. Then as now, families tended to be large, as clans sought to raise soldiers and workers who would replace those taken in war, forced into servitude, or were killed in blood feuds.

The Shkumbin River has traditionally divided the northern Ghegs from the southern Tosks. Though both groups speak the Albanian language of Shqip, their dialects differ.

The Ghegs are mountain people who even during Ottoman rule preserved a clan-oriented society. The clan was ruled by a tribal chief, but all were equal under his rule. A small minority of the Ghegs were Roman Catholic, but most were Sunni Muslim. Though they supported Albanian independence, their enthusiasm was tempered by a fear that a strong central government would erode tribal authority. This authority was codified in the Kanun, a 15th century system of governance written by an Albanian chieftain named Lek Dukagjin. The Kanun was interpreted by the tribal chief, and its precepts even today form the basis of family and clan expectations, and thus of Albanian life.

The Tosks, living south of the Shkumbin River, have had more contact with people from outside the country because of their more accessible terrain. Though Tosks also were tribal people, the Ottoman influence was more strongly felt here. The Tosks were also primarily Muslim, but their community included Bektashi Muslims as well as Sunni. The Bektashi Muslims were more tolerant of other religions and helped set a tolerant tone for Tosks, who also included in their number Eastern Orthodox Christians, who would later form the Albanian Orthodox Church.

Ghegs tend to be more animated than the Tosks, arguing vociferously and appearing angry to outsiders. Traditionally, it is the Ghegs who supplied the armies with their soldiers and whose personalities and demeanor even today recall the fierce soldiers they once were. The Tosks, who were farmers, are somewhat quieter and less boisterous.

THE ALBANIAN CHARACTER

At the time of Albanian independence in 1912, nearly 90 percent of the people were rural. Only three cities in Albania had more than 10,000 people, and the largest was Shkodra with 25,000. It was within the clans and rural communities that most people developed their sense of themselves as Albanians and this self-image has not changed over the centuries.

Adversity has shaped a character strong on loyalty and stoicism. Many Albanians have been raised by their parents to expect a war for each generation. In the face of such hardship, they remain generous and willing to share what they have with visitors or fellow Albanians in need.

An Albanian man plays with his grandchildren outside his home.

The Albanian character

Central to an Albanian's self-image is the concept of the *besa* (BEH-sah), or "word of honor." An Albanian proverb says "An honest man will not break his word," and this is the cornerstone of the Albanian character. Besa, as it is called in Shqip, confers the absolute certainty that what has been promised will be delivered. As part of the Kanun, besa survived the best efforts of the Turks and the Communists to replace it with their own certainties. Besa regulated business transactions, marriage proposals, and all acts of faith both between individuals and groups such as families and clans. With a population that was largely illiterate, besa was crucial to society at every level. Not only was it a matter of personal honor, but it was enforced by the group as well. Violating besa was punishable by death, and the shame and resulting consequences could extend to the whole family and beyond. The duty to avenge a violation of besa also applied to the extended family and was one of the causes of blood feuds extending for generations. Even today, Albanians are not likely to say they will do something they are not sure they can do.

Albanians are fervent handshakers. Visitors, whether friend or family, must shake hands with the host at the door and, once inside, with everyone present—beginning with the eldest and working down. Close friends may kiss on the cheek, but only within gender. Once seated, the guest will be told, "You are welcome here," and will reply, "It is a pleasure to be here." On the street, Albanians shake hands every time they meet.

The communal nature of life under communism has led Albanians to expect less privacy and to offer less privacy than Westerners are accustomed to. A foreigner is of great interest to many Albanians, and they will not hesitate to interrupt a conversation among people they do not know.

"Who builds with sweat, defends with blood."

—*Albanian proverb*

BALKANS, BALKANIZE: THE EVOLUTION OF A WORD

The Balkan Mountains in Bulgaria give their name to a large peninsula in Europe called the Balkan Peninsula. The countries on and near the Balkan Peninsula are referred to collectively as the Balkan countries. Before the 20th century these countries were parts of the Roman and Greek Empires, the Ottoman Empire, and the Hapsburg Dynasty among others. In the 20th century two wars were fought over these territories, resulting in a division of lands and of people of strong ethnic, religious, and national loyalties.

Until the 1990s these countries, except for Albania, were under the control of the Soviet Union. With the collapse of the Soviet Union these countries were theoretically free to go their own way. But they remained haunted by the ethnic divisions that had been submerged under totalitarian rule, and these divisions emerged in full view of the whole world in the horrors of murderous purges called ethnic cleansing.

By the end of the 20th century Balkanize was a verb known to all as the process of carving up a territory into small states at war with their neighbors and with themselves. Today balkanize refers to a more generalized process of putting members of a group, a team, or even a family at odds with each other by setting them in competition with each other rather than in pursuit of group goals.

JEWS

There are no longer any Jews in Albania, but there were through World War II. Their story is a tribute to the character of Albanians. Like other occupied countries in Europe, Albania was ordered by the fascists to round up and deport their Jewish citizens to extermination sites outside the country. Rather than comply, Albanians sheltered their Jewish neighbors, hiding them in attics and barns until the end of the war, telling the Nazis that there were no Jews in Albania. When the war ended, the Jews of Albania, some 300 of them, emigrated as a group to Palestine.

ROMA

Roma, or Gypsies, are nomadic in Albania, as they are, or were, in many countries in Europe. Though they are officially counted as less than 2 percent of the population, their nomadic existence makes them unreliably available to census counters, and that number is certainly lower than it should be. The children are everywhere in the cities, often begging for change from visitors.

ETHNICITY

A Roma family.

Ethnicity in Albania is a subject for political cautiousness. Under communism, of course, no mention or recognition of ethnic identity was allowed. With 95 percent of the population ethnic Albanian, the remaining 5 percent might logically seem unimportant. However, in the Balkan countries, ethnicity is always important because people are loyal to the country of their ethnicity. In Albania, this means Greece and Serbia, primarily, countries with a history of enmity toward Albania and toward Albanians in their countries. To minimize problems, Albania did not in its last census ask any questions that would identify ethnicity or first language. Therefore there are no accurate numbers.

It is illegal for a political party to identify itself with one ethnic group. The Human Rights Union Party (PBDNj) represents the minority groups in Albania, with the majority of its power coming from the Greek population. In 2001 it received 2.5 percent of the vote, which gave it three seats in the People's Assembly.

DUAL NATIONALITY

Under current Albanian law any person of Albanian parentage in the country is considered to be Albanian. This applies to visitors or citizens of other countries as well. Albanian males who have emigrated to other countries may be considered to be draft evaders if they have not fulfilled their compulsory military obligation. If they are caught while visiting Albania, they may be arrested and prosecuted in an Albanian court, even if they have become citizens elsewhere.

ALBANIAN ICONS

Every town and city of any size has a statue of George "Skenderbeg," Kastrioti, a street named after him, a square known as Skenderbeg Square, or all three. No matter who is in charge of Albania, Skenderbeg is always beloved and admired. During the reign of Enver Hoxha, Hoxha's own pictures and statues were even more ubiquitous than Skenderbeg's.

Albanians saw his face everywhere they turned, and in some towns many of the streets bore his name. If that was confusing, no one dared say.

When Hoxha died, he was buried in a prominent position, with a large red marble headstone and two guards perpetually stationed at his grave. In 1992 his body was exhumed and moved to a less prestigious spot. As in many countries released from a dictator's tyranny, people pulled down his statues and defaced paintings and posters.

Albanians have supplied soldiers and leaders throughout the Balkans and Italy for centuries. Both the Romans and Turks recognized the ancestors of modern-day Albanians for their military courage and intelligence as soldiers in their armies. The *sipahis* (see-PAH-his), as the Albanian army units were known, fought ferociously and effectively in Turkish campaigns through the 16th and 17th centuries. Many parts of the Ottoman Empire were ruled by Albanian pashas and grand viziers (similar to prime ministers) to Turkish sultans.

In Italy, which has had an Albanian community of refugees called the Arberesh since the 15th century, Albanians have provided a pope and three cardinals to the Roman Catholic Church and a prime minister, Francesco Crispi, to the government. Napoleon's mother was Albanian, as were Ataturk, the founder of the modern Turkish state, and Mehemet Ali considered the founder of modern Egypt.

LIFESTYLE

Until the 20th century when communism created an Albanian sense of nationality, people in the mountains of the north, the Ghegs, gave their loyalty to kinship groups and within these clans to their families. Extended families, consisting of parents and their sons and their families, and unmarried daughters, usually lived together. The families formed an individual and usually independent residential and economic unit. Individual families could consist of as many as 60 members, who lived in small dwellings around the parents' larger home. The governing organization was the clan, and the clan leader settled disputes, arranged marriages, and determined the hierarchy within the group. Disputes that could not be settled by his intervention became blood feuds, which carried through to succeeding generations, sometimes to be continued in exile in other countries.

Left: **The elderly who live in smaller towns spend much of their time socializing, playing cards, or just talking.**

Opposite: **Rearing livestock, such as cows and sheep, is a way of life for many rural Albanians.**

In the southern part of the country lived the Tosks. They were mostly Muslim, but the comparative accessibility of their terrain had left them less isolated and more open to outside influences. Though they, too, had tribal loyalties, these ties had been somewhat weakened by the feudal rule of the Turkish aristocracy. Their independence, like their isolation, was less complete.

Both Tosks and Ghegs gave complete authority to the father as head of the family. Marriages were arranged in infancy, usually outside the clan. Failure to carry through on the arranged marriages would result in a blood feud. Upon the death of the father, the oldest son assumed leadership of the family, but the family's assets were divided among all the sons. Women were not allowed to own anything or to seek divorce.

These children in Tirana are learning to play the violin at age 6.

BLOOD AND SUGAR

A blood feud is a dispute between two families or clans over a perceived matter of honor for which blood revenge (usually meaning the murder of a member of the opposing family) must be sought. Among the mountain people blood from a murdered clan or family member was put in a small vial. Here it would remain till it began to ferment. At that point, the family would declare that the murdered one's "blood is boiling," and they would go out and take their revenge.

Another tradition involving blood is the ceremony that makes two men blood brothers. They will each draw

blood by cutting their own arms. They put some of the blood on a lump of sugar, and then each man eats the sugar of the other.

Children were raised to respect their father and obey him without question. Any insult to the father would also result in a blood feud. Women were treated as servants and kept separate from the men.

Historically, Albanians have felt safe only inside their homes, and that feeling has not changed with the events of the last century. An Albanian home will be clean and calm, with books, a computer, and a television like many European homes. This is a great contrast, though, to the scene outside the home in most Albanian cities, where trash litters the streets, factories stand empty, traffic is unregulated and terrifying, and crime is uncontrolled. Though the country is in transition, the Albanian home remains the center of life. Sundays are reserved for the family, and guests who are invited to share that day with an Albanian family have been truly honored.

Above: **Family ties are strong among Albanians. If one member of the family is wronged, it is expected that another will take revenge.**

RURAL LIFE

In Muslim communities women are expected to stay at home. Their lives are quite separate from those of the men. They usually rise early to make their family's breakfast. For the rest of the day, they clean and prepare the afternoon meal. It is a point of pride for Albanians that their homes are scrupulously clean. Water and electricity are not reliably available, so cleaning and preparing the afternoon meal, which is the main meal of the day, can be very labor intensive. Girls are expected to stay home as well, helping the women with the work of the house and learning how to take care of their own houses when they are grown.

After their breakfast, men begin their day in the village. They spend much of their time strolling around town with their friends or sitting in the cafés drinking coffee or the Albanian national drink, raki, a Turkish liqueur. The Muslims of Albania identify themselves strongly as Muslim, but they do not observe the dietary laws, and liquor is freely available and consumed. Boys are free to play with their friends or go to the cafés with the men. If classes are available, they will spend some time in school each day.

The evenings are often graced with visits. Friends and family drop in for a cup of Turkish coffee and to renew old acquaintances. Without telephones in most homes, this is how many Albanians keep in touch with each other and share the news of their lives. To visit is to confer honor on the host, so most visits are considered formal affairs even within small groups, and the coffee is served in the best cups.

Hospitality is a virtue and a source of pride. Albanians will always pick up a check for their guest for coffee and drinks. Guests in the home will be offered food and drink, usually both coffee and raki, and will be expected to accept. Albanians even drink raki in the morning, as a breakfast beverage. Still, they are not heavy drinkers, and public drunkenness is a source of shame.

CITY LIFE

A day in the city is not too much different from a day in the village. Here, too, people rise very early to make sure that there will be hot water and electricity for their morning needs. Sometimes it is necessary to draw the water at certain times of the day, such as 4:00 A.M., 1:00 P.M., and 7:00 P.M. because that is when it is available. City dwellers fill pots and tubs, then heat the water when they need it. Tap water must be boiled before drinking.

After breakfast, people leave for school or work—if either is available. Even at that early hour vendors are selling raki as well as Turkish coffee on the streets. Most people come home for the noon meal. Though it is not official, many businesses and offices shut down for a few hours in the early afternoon, reopening late in the afternoon for a short time. This habit is traditional in some of the surrounding countries, especially Italy, but it is also necessary because there is not much work and there are few customers in the shops due to the poor economy.

For many Albanians, the xhiro (ZEE-rroh), the walk about town, is the high point of every day. In the early evening, groups of mostly boys and men dress in their finest clothes and walk around the center of the town for an hour or more.

Opposite: **A group of men on their way to the center of town for the daily xhiro.**

A traditional home in a rural part of Albania. In contrast to the chaos outside, Albanian homes are clean and calm and are one place where the people feel most secure.

SAFETY AND SECURITY FOR ALBANIANS

Safety and stability have improved in this century in Albania, but a high crime rate still exists—especially for armed robbery, sexual assault, and car theft. Organized crime and corruption, while not necessarily affecting daily life, do decrease the likelihood that victims of crimes will find redress for wrongs done to them. People are, therefore, not inclined to travel outside cities after dark and are warned to avoid large crowds.

EDUCATION

Schooling is not universally available, although over 80 percent of children under ten years of age are in school. Most government classes have between 40 and 50 students. Teacher education, salaries, and support have plummeted. The educational opportunities have declined since the fall of communism, under which everyone received free education until age eighteen and many received free college or technical education as well. When the communist government fell, rioters destroyed many of the schools, and each government failure has led to more destruction. Today, foreigners brought in by international relief agencies teach many classes. The children show an enthusiasm for Western action movie stars of the past century like Sylvester Stallone and Jean-Claude Van Damme, and, of course, soccer stars. Many already plan to emigrate.

Under communism the literacy rate was nearly 100 percent. Today, it is no more than 88 percent, a substantial decline and the lowest literacy rate in Europe.

Young children attending class in Tirana.

YOUNG ADULTS

Since 1992, 20 percent of Albania's young people have emigrated. For those who remain, life is challenging. Educational opportunities are fewer and often of questionable quality since the collapse of communism. The dropout rate has risen, and the enrollment rate has declined. Economic and social problems make educational access unequal, and although 90 percent of school-age children were said to be attending school in 2000, the number of teachers has decreased and their qualifications are often questionable.

The opening of the borders has exposed Albania's young people to increased danger of HIV/AIDS infection and drug abuse. Unemployment has given rise to drug and human trafficking, prostitution, and other criminal activities. In these spheres young people are both the criminals and the victims.

Even in the last years of communism, the government recognized the disaffection of its young people and the risk their alienation posed to the country. Its rollback of restrictions in the late 1980s, though not enough to save the system, was aimed mainly at appeasing the youth, who were responding more than their elders to the news from outside that a new day was coming. For many the day did not come fast enough, and they have emigrated; but both the Albanian government and international relief agencies from Italy, France, the United States, and the United Nations have developed programs to

When not at work, these young men spend their free time catching up with friends at the local café.

educate and train the young people who remain, in an effort to use their energy to rebuild Albania.

The Muslim separation of the sexes does not have nearly as tight a hold on the young people in the cities. Discos and cafés are gathering places where young men and women meet and hang out. Though raves are rare, there are enough clubs and dance halls that play dance music and dj mixes of underground, techno, breaks, and chill, sounds familiar to those in the know.

THE INTERNET

Twenty years ago, poverty and technical backwardness might have perpetuated the isolation the communists imposed on Albania. But today there is the Internet. With more Albanians outside of Albania than within the country, communication is necessary to preserve family and ethnic ties. Numerous sites on the Internet keep Albanians around the world in touch with each other and provide outsiders with information they would otherwise have trouble finding, since Albania is not yet a travel destination of choice for many. Young people abroad for work or education communicate by e-mail with their friends back home who have access to their own computers, which were brought home or ordered from other countries, or who frequent the Internet cafés, which are becoming more prevalent in the cities. Computer access is not as ubiquitous as in other European cities, and deficiencies in the electrical and telecommunication systems hamper users. But for those who successfully make the effort, it has been a lifeline to the outside world.

A woman herds a flock of turkeys.

WOMEN

Traditionally, women in Albania have had two faces. One was the face of a beautiful creature lauded in legend and poetry. The other face was the mother and wife who bore, fed, and clothed her family and worked in the fields with her husband, maintaining the traditions and values handed down to her. As a free and strong spirit, the first face inspired dreams and art. The second face was restricted to the home, taking no part in the social or political lives of men.

Though the communist regime that dominated Albania for over half a century brought repression and terror to the people, it also brought equality of opportunity and education. Women were paid equally for their work and held 30 percent of government positions. Girls, as well as boys, were given at least eight years of education and equal opportunities for advanced education and training. Women soon became more productive than men and accounted for 80 percent of the light industrial workers and those who work in the field of education.

Since the fall of communism most of these women have become unemployed. The numbers in the professions and government have fallen dramatically, and many women are again restricted to a life in the home. In the rural areas women once again work the land, which has been privatized and divided into smallholdings. Their work is especially arduous, since the equipment is either outdated, worn-out, or nonexistent. Many of the husbands and fathers have emigrated in search of employment, leaving the women to do their work as well.

The equality bestowed by the Communists had shallow roots and no tradition behind it. Today, religious tradition has taken its place and women no longer compete on equal footing. Some have organized and tried to assert themselves in favor of social change and equality, but in an economy with mass unemployment, job equality is a small prize. Where schools are unstaffed or closed, educational equality does not bring education.

Still, the women of Albania have fought before. In World War II more than 6,000 women out of a population of less than one million fought in the resistance against the fascists. Today, the Independent Forum for Albanian Women addresses the special needs of a country in transition. They are working to identify the problems unique to women in Albania and to develop projects to meet these needs. At the same time, other women's groups are working to regain some of the political power they have lost, organizing women's parties to run for office.

Today, as in the past, young women who are in the military help to keep Albania safe.

81

RELIGION

FOR HUNDREDS OF YEARS, Albania was a country that tolerated a multiplicity of religions—Christianity, Islam, and Judaism. In 1967 it declared atheism its national "religion" and outlawed and repressed any other religious practice. After a few years of regenerated practice, religions of all sorts thrived in Albania, enriching the spiritual life of the people. Local and international religious organizations contribute valuable educational and social services to the country in its time of transition. Many have taken Albania's prior atheism as a spiritual challenge, and the country is regarded as a hot spot for Christian missionary work. Scholars estimate that roughly 70 percent of the people were Muslim, 20 percent Orthodox Christian, and 10 percent Roman Catholic in the first half of the 20th century. With religion repressed for over 40 years and outlawed for nearly 25 of those years, many people have no tradition at all of a theistic belief.

Left: **The remains of a Byzantine church and a medieval monastery in the ancient site of Apollonia, located in the Fierit region.**

Opposite: **The prayer room in the Etem Bey mosque in Tirana is intricately decorated.**

During Hoxha's rule, this cathedral was converted into a cinema. After the fall of communism it was converted back into a cathedral where Masses are held regularly, even though construction is still ongoing.

ATHEISM

When Enver Hoxha outlawed religion in 1967, he destroyed or converted into storage places, sports arenas, and public toilets 2,169 mosques, monasteries, and churches. A law prohibiting religious practices prescribed long prison sentences for those who transgressed and public execution for those who tried to leave the country. Every religious and cultural value connected with the past was erased from public consciousness. Religious scholars and leaders were imprisoned, executed, or forced to renounce their beliefs.

A whole generation grew up without faith, without seeing a mosque or a church. Worshipping privately was also dangerous because secret police were everywhere and neighbors were obliged to spy on each other. Yet religion remained deep in the hearts of some of the people. Islamic ceremonies were organized in secret. The faithful fasted during the holy Ramadan month without calling attention to themselves. Likewise, Christians held secret communion services and privately familiarized themselves with Bible stories.

Albanian religious practices have a pragmatic side that reflects the history of believers in a hostile atmosphere. Since religious practice was illegal and, therefore, very dangerous for more than 20 years, Muslims minimized the outward manifestations of their beliefs. As a result, many devout Muslims in Albania today do not observe either dietary laws or the requirements that they pray five times a day.

This tradition of accommodating the enemy has a Christian equivalent as well. During the Turkish occupation Christianity was tolerated in

an otherwise Muslim land. However, Christians were required to surrender one of their sons for military duty and to pay taxes that were not demanded of Muslims. To save their sons and their money, many Christians converted to Islam, and others pretended to convert, practicing their own faith in secret.

After communism fell, the old mosques and churches were reopened as places of worship. Those destroyed were rebuilt or replaced as money allowed. The Albanian Muslim community took shape and coalesced around its spiritual leader, Hafiz Sabri Koci Effendi, who emerged as the grand mufti after languishing in communist prisons for 25 years. New magazines and newspapers have begun being published. Some 25 Muslim organizations are active and engaged in rebuilding mosques in villages and cities.

This warehouse in Shkodra was converted into a mosque after the fall of communism.

CHRISTIANITY

Christianity has had followers in Albania since the fourth century, when the Ghegs in the north became Roman Catholics and the Tosks in the south converted to Christianity. Albanians, both at home and in exile, had wanted to establish an Orthodox Church independent of Greek, Turkish, or Serbian authority since the 1880s.

Exiles in the United States especially encouraged the development of a church with Albanian priests and an Albanian liturgy. This could not happen in Albania before independence, because the Turks wanted to

Easter mass being celebrated at a church that was destroyed during the time when Albania was under communist rule.

keep control of the Church. Therefore, the first Albanian Orthodox Church was founded in Boston, Massachusetts, in 1908, initially as a mission of the Russian Orthodox Church and then, in 1919, as an Albanian diocese of its own.

As an independent diocese, the Albanian Orthodox Church took on a patriotic role as well as a spiritual one. Its first priest, Fan S. Noli, an Albanian expatriate living in Boston, translated the service and the liturgical books into Albanian and used the pulpit to preach the word of Albanian independence as well as the word of God.

As a religious institution, the church was of interest mainly to Orthodox Albanians, but its insistence on loosening the ties of authority from both Greece and Turkey found favor with Catholics and Muslims as well, both within Albania and in the outlying expatriate communities around the world. Albanians of all faiths recognized the significance when the patriarch of Constantinople declared the Albanian Orthodox Church fully independent in 1937.

The savage repression of religion from 1949 to 1990 left the Albanian Orthodox Church without leaders. All the bishops had been killed or had died in prison or in exile. As it struggled to reestablish itself the church once again was strife ridden, as Greek and Turkish Orthodox authorities tried once again to take control. By 1998, though, ethnic Albanians were once again in leadership positions in their own church with an archbishop and three bishops. Today, it claims a membership of 160,000.

In the years after the church emerged from what Albanians called "the atheist dungeon," 70 new churches were built and 163 repaired or reclaimed. A theological academy opened in Durres in an abandoned hotel, with a student enrollment of 60 young men preparing for the priesthood.

My dearest People of Albania! The news of the trouble that has come to our wonderful country has caused me great sorrow . . . Mother is praying much for all my dear people of Albania, that each one will learn to love until it hurts and so bring peace to the country and to each heart. Let us pray. God bless you.

—Mother Teresa, letter written to the Albanian people on hearing of the violence following the collapse of the pyramid scheme. April 28, 1997, Tirana

FOLK BELIEFS

Besides religious beliefs, Albanians have a rich tradition of folktales and legends that embody some of the beliefs and moral attitudes that enrich their lives and shape their character. These stories, many collected by philologists during the 19th century, survived the vicissitudes of the 20th century and are still told in the villages in the evenings. Like folktales the world over, Albanian stories center on the struggle between the forces of good and evil, but their influences reflect Albania's history of invasion and occupation. Though the setting is usually European, the characters include dervishes and pashas indicative of the country's Ottoman history. Two folk heroes, Mujo and Halil, are familiar to old folks and children alike, from stories and songs sung in the mountain villages of the north, where these heroes roamed with their band of adventurers.

One folk custom reflects the importance that rain played in the lives of a people who were almost all farmers. In times of drought, a young boy or girl who had been chosen as *dordolec* (dor-DOH-leck), or rainmaker, would go around the countryside singing:

Dordolec, dordolec, bring the rain
For our corn upon the plain
Three ears on every stalk!
Rain in May
A golden tray.

Rain in June
A pretty tune.
July rain
A brimful wine.
August rain
Bushels of grain.

ISLAM

The religion of Islam is complex and varied in its manifestations. Like Muslims everywhere, the Muslims of Albania follow the teachings of the Koran, the writings of Muhammad. They believe that Muhammad is the prophet of God. Beyond that belief, though, Albanians remain quite independent in their beliefs and practices. As a group, Albanian Muslims, both in and outside the country, resist a tendency toward the fundamentalism of countries such as Saudi Arabia and parts of Iraq. Having lived under the most rigorous totalitarianism in which both democracy and religion were banned, they are inclined to value both their religious heritage and a democratic government.

Nor are Albanians likely to allow foreigners to tell them that their customs must be abandoned and their behavior determined by Islamic totalitarians. They believe in the validity of their own history, their own

culture, and their own Albanian model of Islam based on interfaith respect and the understanding that religion is private. In the international controversy over the future of Islam, Albanians feel compelled to reinforce Albanian values. This means that as Muslims, they must love both Allah and their neighbors.

Albanian Muslims have been criticized by fundamentalists in the Middle East for their support of and participation in the coalition that invaded Iraq in 2003. Yet they have made their position clear: their support extends beyond words to the commitment of troops.

Albanians—with an isolated culture, a language without close relatives, and a tradition of avoiding religious differences in the interest of national unity—are generally wary of outsiders. Their identity as Muslims and as Albanians is a topic that intrigues many Albanian young people. With unemployment high and the future uncertain, Albanians do not want a reputation for Islamic extremism. As young people with a European future in a free-market country and a sexually egalitarian past under communism, they are particularly conflicted about the repression of women.

Muslim men in Albania praying with rosaries in a mosque.

LANGUAGE

THE ALBANIAN LANGUAGE, Shqip, is spoken by over five million people throughout Albania and the lands to which Albanians have relocated. The origins of Shqip are unknown, but most scholars believe that it derives from Illyrian languages spoken in Albania over 2,000 years ago. It is not related to any other Indo-European language, making it unique and largely unintelligible to speakers from other countries. However, speakers of the two dialects have no trouble understanding each other.

The earliest references to an Albanian language come from travelers from other lands in the 14th century. These travelers noted that the language was different from the Greek, Latin, and Slavic tongues spoken throughout the area and that none of the speakers of those languages could understand Albanian. Although the language seems to have been well established by then, no written examples of it remain.

Left: **This university class for ethnic Albanians in Kosovo is conducted in Shqip.**

Opposite: **A billboard with text in the Albanian language of Shqip. The language has two separate dialects. Tosk is spoken in southern Albania and by Albanians in Greece. Gheg is the dialect of the north and of Kosovo, Macedonia, and Montenegro.**

Above: **A page from the *Meshari*.**

Opposite: **Two Albanians in a café share a story.**

MESHARI

The earliest known book written in Shqip is a religious book called *Meshari*, meaning missal, by Gjon Buzuku, a Catholic cleric, probably from northern Albania. The Vatican Library has the only known existing copy of the book, originally a 188-page volume, with many illustrations and illuminated letters. The first 16 pages and the frontispiece are missing, so its exact date of publication is unknown; but it is believed to be 1555. Today, a publishing house in Prishtina, Kosovo, is named after Gjon Buzuku.

Meshari has been valuable to scholars and historians because so much of its text is familiar. It consists largely of translations of texts that are known from other contexts, such as the New Testament of the Bible and Catholic liturgical prayers and rituals. The language patterns of the text have much to tell about Shqip as it existed during the time *Meshari* was written.

ALBANIAN SAYINGS AND PROVERBS

The sayings and proverbs of Albania are unique, if often puzzling to outsiders. Many of them center on being prepared for adversity. Others promote courage or justify ferocity.

Do not hide like a fly under the tail of a horse. (from Korce)
You cannot catch a flea with gloves. (from Korce)
If you do not have malice inside, it will not come from outside. (from Vlona and Berat)
You cannot hunt with a tied dog. (from Kruja)
The wolf has a thick neck because it has fast legs.
No bird flies around in threes.
When a man and a dog go for a walk on a leash, the man may think he is leading, but the dog goes first.

Albanians also delight in what can best be called contemporary proverbs. Though expressed in the oblique style of the traditional proverbs and sayings, they have a decidedly current edge:

The safest place to grow marijuana is in the policeman's garden.
"Ordnance survey" does not sound as sinister as "military map," but they mean the same thing.

ALPHABET SOUP

Throughout the centuries of Turkish domination, the Albanians maintained their spoken language. In the 19th century they even began to publish books in Albanian, though the alphabet was not yet codified, and to teach their children in Albanian-language schools. They persisted in their use of Shqip both within and outside Albania despite opposition from the Turks, as well as from Greece, Serbia, and Montenegro.

The Albanian alphabet is based on the Latin alphabet with several additional letters to accommodate some uniquely Shqip sounds. It consists of 36 letters. Not all of them have English sound equivalents, the closest being Spanish or French. The Albanian alphabet as it exists today took some time to evolve and coalesce. In 1824 Naum Veqilharxhi developed an alphabet he called Evetor in an effort to free the language of Greek and

Posted on the fence of a Kosovar refugee camp, this notice is written in both English and Albanian. It is an appeal from an ethnic Albanian who had fled Kosovo for the whereabouts of his missing family.

Latin influences. Other alphabets in use at the time included Arabic, and Greek-influenced versions, and one called Istanbul. Several literary societies developed their own alphabets as well.

By the 20th century it was becoming clear that a country as tiny as Albania was not well served by upward of ten alphabets, and so in 1908 the Alphabet Congress was convened. For the next three years controversy prevented settling on just one alphabet. Catholics felt their teachings could only be rendered in a Latin-based alphabet, while a group called the Young Turks maintained that a non-Islamic alphabet violated Islamic law. In cities throughout the country, people demonstrated in favor of their alphabetic choice. In 1911 the Young Turks, who had been told by their clerics that they would be considered infidels if they used the Latin alphabet, nevertheless dropped their objections and the script used today was adopted. It is called Bashkimi, meaning "union," and is named after the literary society that developed it.

Armouniams, or Vlachs, a nomadic people of southeastern Albania, speak a language related to Romanian. Roma speak their own language, Romany. Because both of these groups are nomadic, their numbers are sometimes underestimated.

At Radio K in Prishtina, Kosovo, Albanians and Serbs work side by side. This radio station broadcasts into Albania.

COMMUNICATING IN ALBANIA

Telephone communication with Albania barely existed before 1990. Political restrictions forbade international telephoning, and poverty and technological backwardness prevented domestic telephoning. In 1990 only one in one hundred Albanians had a phone. With the overthrow of the communist government, progress in telephone communication was expected, but civil unrest throughout the 1990s resulted in an actual decline, as people in the countryside tore down and used the telephone lines to build fences. The telephone lines in Albania are outdated and damaged, but cellular phones have improved access for people in the cities.

Nearly one in three people has a radio and television in Albania. The country has 17 radio stations and three television broadcasting stations. Radio and television broadcasts from other countries are also available. In 2001 ten thousand people were hooked up to the Internet, and the number has more than tripled since then. Reception of all these services is sometimes shut down when electricity is limited or unavailable.

A COUNTRY OF MANY LANGUAGES

Albanians take pride in the uniqueness of their language and in its reputation for difficulty. Still, visitors don't usually have trouble communicating because so many Albanians speak more than one language. Some speak English, mostly younger people who may speak three or four languages. The most widely spoken foreign language is

Italian because of the Italian TV stations that have been widely accessible since the Communist days. In the south of the country, many people speak Greek, and along the Serbian border some speak Serbo-Croatian. Older Albanians may have learned Russian in the days of Albania's alliance with the Soviet Union, but they probably haven't had good reason to speak it for many years. During the 1950s, while Albania and China enjoyed good relations, people who are now middle-aged studied in China under cultural exchange programs. Today, after a long absence, these programs have resumed, and young Albanians are once again studying in China and learning Chinese.

Men in Albania buying newspapers from a street vendor.

ARTS

THE OLDEST ALBANIAN EPICS featured heroic noblemen, fairies, and gods. More recent epics, originating during the Turkish occupation, tell of resistance and freedom fighters. These stories were written down for the first time in the 1950s. Until then, they existed in the oral tradition, part song and part tale, performed at community ceremonies and family gatherings. In earlier times they were performed by traveling singer-poets who were welcomed into the communities as wise and accomplished men. In addition to preserving the heroic tales, Albanian epics also reinforced traditional values such as the sanctity of the tribe and family, the importance of the promise, and the necessity of the blood feud in the defense of honor and family.

These are values that to this day define Albanians, some of whom can recite in detail wrongs done to their families in the two world wars.

The Stalinist purges of intellectuals in Albania after World War II nearly brought to a halt any new literature and much consideration of the literature of the past. But in 1961, after Albania broke off ties with the Soviet Union, a new Albanian nationalism gave rise to a desire among the people for artistic expression. Though the government permitted only works of social realism that celebrated the communist cause and its values, artists were able, as they often are in totalitarian states, to express themselves obliquely and subtly.

Above: **A monument to Lord Byron of Britain who had spent some time in Albania.**

Opposite: **Skenderbeg's Museum in Kruja is home to these elaborate representations of his heroic battles.**

ISMAIL KADARE

Ismail Kadare, born in 1930, grew to maturity under communist rule. Throughout his early career his writing moved subtly away from the demands of social realism and his reputation grew within his own country. In 1963 he published his first major novel in French. *The General of the Dead Army*, as it is called in English, brought him an international reputation that made his position in Albania somewhat more secure, and he continued to write in both French and Albanian. Most of his novels written during that time have since been translated into English including *Chronicle in Stone*, 1987; *Broken April*, 1990; and *The Palace of Dreams*, 1993.

By 1990 Kadare's work had caused enough displeasure among the authorities that he could no longer work and live with any degree of safety within Albania. Just months before the collapse of the regime, he fled to France, where he was granted political asylum. Since the fall of communism he has maintained a dual citizenship, and spends time in both countries.

In his work Kadare's artistic and intellectual restlessness has brought to the forefront the complexity of life under tyranny. He has maintained that an "inner freedom" is of primary artistic importance and can thrive under the most dire political circumstances.

FATOS LUBONJA

Literature in Albania has blossomed since the fall of communism. Some of its vitality has been made possible by the Internet. Fatos Lubonja, a writer and editor living in Tirana, has a well-established reputation in Albania as an activist and intellectual. His work is available internationally through the organization called Words Without Borders. His story *Ahlem* is a moving account of the difficulties of surviving in the prisons of Albania's past. The story tells of the poisonous effects on the spirit of betrayal, mistrust, and false hope, and yet it is a story of survival.

Fatos Lubonja himself is a survivor of the world and experiences that he writes about in *Ahlem*. Born in 1951 into a family already active in resistance to the government, Fatos at the age of 23 was sentenced to seven years imprisonment for keeping a diary that contained what the government called "agitation and propaganda." Four years into his sentence, Lubonja was sentenced to another 25 years for "counter-revolutionary activity." He has written an account of his experience in *The Second Sentence*, a documentary novel dedicated to the nine other prisoners who were tried with him. Lubonja was released in 1991, after serving 17 years of his sentence. Today, he publishes *Perpjekja*, meaning "Endeavor," a quarterly journal of stories, poetry, and essays of cultural and political criticism. Lubonja has done much to encourage his fellow Albanians to work for change and progress through dissent and discussion rather than violence and destruction.

Liri Lubonja, Fatos's mother, was sent into internal exile while her husband and son were imprisoned. She, too, has written a book, Far Away Among People, *which tells the stories of the people in the village where she was interned.*

THE VISUAL ARTS

The visual arts in Albania have for centuries been a reflection of the ethnic and religious culture of its people.

Early Illyrians left tiny metal figurines and pottery that recent archaeological digs have retrieved. Other metalwork and pottery show the Illyrians to have been skilled metalworkers and potters, as well as stonecutters, leather workers, and weavers. Medieval painters and metalworkers produced icons of exceptional beauty. The city of Elbasan recorded over 45 craft guilds in the 17th century where trained artisans produced leather goods, textiles, jewelry, and silver goods to export throughout the Ottoman Empire.

The 17th century painter Onufri is one of Albania's most celebrated artists. His Christian icons show his skill as a master dyemaker as well as painter. His representational skill and use of color are equally deft. Some of Onufri's icons are embellished with hammered gold filigree.

Johannes Cetiri, a 17th-century painter from Korce, painted scenes of the city of Berat. His style shows a movement towards realism. The late 19th and early 20th centuries brought impressionism to Albania, and the works of the artist Zaimi show the influence of the French together with the unique perspective of Albania.

The communist government was more inclined to put its people to work on farms and in factories than in artist collectives, but statuary was a notable exception. Throughout Albania statues of Enver Hoxha and other communist leaders were ubiquitous. Since the fall of communism they have been preserved in museums but are no longer visible anywhere else.

Since 1990, the freedom to work in any medium and to represent any subject has resulted in a rebirth of painting and a move into multimedia art. Young artists working in Albania show their work at fairs and festivals and, increasingly, on the Internet.

Opposite: **A mural from a Christian church.**

Below: **The National Culture Museum's façade pays tribute to Albania's workforce.**

FILM

Albania does not have a video rental industry, but movies are often pirated and made available on the black market to people with video machines. The government does not enforce copyright laws, so television stations broadcast many recent movie releases. This makes them accessible to many TV viewers, but it leaves the film industry particularly unprofitable.

That Albania even has a film industry is surprising considering the lack of money available for what might be considered a luxury. In addition, people available for crew work were trained on now obsolete Russian and Chinese equipment, and there are no film schools in the country. Making matters even worse, many movie theaters have closed because they were unprofitable.

And yet the Albanian film industry succeeds because of the unique perspective of its filmmakers. Funding, training, and technical support and equipment have come from partnerships with French film houses, and Albania has recently made several award winning films. One, called *Slogans*, was released in 2001. The producing of this film illustrates how this international cooperation works to keep a small industry alive under difficult conditions. The movie, like many Albanian films, was based on a novel. *The Stone Slogans* by Ylljet Alicka had been published in France as well as in Albania, so it had some international regard. Because there are no film schools in Albania to produce screenwriters, the novelist worked with a Belgian screenwriter, Yves Hancher, to transform the novel into a screenplay. After the film was made, with French technical assistance and money, the French producers distributed the

Filmmakers were present at the wedding of King Zog in April 1938.

movie in France, while the Albanian producers distributed it in Albania. *Slogans* was shown at Cannes as part of the Director's Fortnight, an offshoot of the Cannes International Film Festival. This showing increased its international reputation, and within a few months it had won several other international prizes.

Like other industries in this transitional country, Albania's film industry will continue to need outside support to succeed. But the vision of the filmmakers and the ideas they bring to their work assure them of continued interest from outside.

Other Albanian films of note are *Tirana Year Zero*, 2001, and *Kolonal Bunker*, 1996.

This movie truck visits the remote villages of the Gjirokastres region to screen the latest Albanian movies.

A group of Albanian musicians practice before a performance. Today's Albanian music, played in clubs, burned on CDs, and transmitted over the Internet, exhibits all the influences of the world community. Young Albanian musicians, like young musicians around the world, record their music and make it available over the Internet to fans and to those they hope will be fans.

MUSIC

Local music was probably once used to accompany rituals of the Illyrian tribes. At that time, the music consisted of a simple melodic line accompanied by drums, chorus, primitive wind instruments made of wood or reed, and maybe a harp.

Despite 500 years of Turkish occupation, Albanians maintained an identity of their own that extends to their musical styles to this day. Though influenced by their occupiers, their music has been that of the Albanian folk, not the Turks. Until around 1945 the only Albanian music that existed had been preserved through the oral folk tradition, as no system of notation or recording had been developed.

Isolation, as in all things Albanian, makes the music of the Ghegs in the north and the Tosks in the south sound very different. The music of the Tosks, in fact, sounds different from just about any other music.

The Tosk traditional polyphonic singing, or part-singing, sounds to the untrained ear as if all the singers are performing different songs that start at a variety of times and proceed to another variety of finishes. This type of music is not unknown in Europe, but it dates back to the earliest forms of polyphonic music, and is not heard elsewhere today. The Ghegs, in contrast, have a mostly monophonic folk tradition, which is more familiar to people in the West.

Albanian music, both instrumental and vocal, features a technique sometimes called gradual pitch blend, which differs from the Western practice of hitting a note precisely on its pitch. Applying this technique to jazz and newer musical forms is considered innovative.

Albania has a rich and varied folk culture with a noticeable difference between the music of the north and the south. In the north the songs are usually sung by one person, and the theme is a heroic endeavor, most often against the Turks. Music in the south of Albania is more communal, often with a chorus. Songs and poems tend to be more lyrical or contemplative than narrative.

A young Albanian man plays the *lahuta*, a lute-like instrument.

Traditional instruments of the area often accompany Albanian folksinging and folk dancing. The most common is the flute, but bagpipes and drums are also heard at many informal gatherings. One instrument, the *lahuta* (LAH-hoo-tah), is a stringed instrument much like the lute that was common in northern Europe during the Renaissance. It is one of the oldest instruments still in use in Europe. The oral poets played the lahuta to call the people to hear their recitations. In the second half of the 20th century, the Institute of Popular Culture in Tirana collected traditional songs, dances, and poetry. Today, it has a collection of about a million verses, 40,000 proverbs, and nearly 10,000 recordings.

LEISURE

LIKE PEOPLE EVERYWHERE, Albanians use much of their spare time to play or watch sports and television. But with family and friends scattered far and wide throughout the world, they place a very high value on keeping in touch. An evening stroll, a visit in the house of friends, or a few hours in a coffeehouse are an important part of the day. Today, the Internet connects many people with friends and family abroad, and they keep track of each other through e-mail.

Opposite: **Albanian children playing in the streets of Tirana.**

Below: **In the summer heat, Albanian children keep cool by swimming.**

SPORTS

The quality of sports and other organized recreational activity has always been linked to the nation's social, political, and economic situation. Between World War II and the 1990s, though Albania's tightly controlled state economy supported sports programs, the nation's lack of economic and social progress resulted in levels of play that failed to rival those of the Soviet Union and other European Communist nations. Since 1990 Albania's emergence from decades of international isolation as an open society has had both rewards and drawbacks for sports fans and athletes.

On the one hand, Albanians have greater variety in the athletic and recreational activities available to them. On the other hand, many Albanians—especially children and young adults—see their newly found political freedom as a chance to leave Albania and live, work, and play abroad.

Despite the problems facing schools that cannot afford organized athletic programs, Albanians enjoy many sports and outdoor activities, such as swimming, hiking, and mountain climbing. Albania also fields players and teams in many sports that involve various levels of national and international competition, including basketball, shooting, volleyball, and—last but certainly not least—soccer.

This junior gymnastics team has to train in an old cathedral that had been converted into a makeshift gymnasium when Albania was under communist rule. The most commonly stated dissatisfaction of young people is the lack of facilities for sports, cultural, and leisure activities, particularly in schools.

BASKETBALL

Although basketball in Albania does not inspire nearly the same passion in its fans as soccer, in the leagues that operate locally and under the auspices of the nation's professional basketball organization, the Basketball

Federation of Albania (BFA), there is no shortage of teams and players to follow. In addition to playing within their own A1 and A2 divisions, the BFA's teams compete within EuroBasket, a confederation of nearly two hundred leagues throughout Europe and neighboring continents.

The A1 division is the BFA's top pro league. Its teams represent most major cities in Albania. Playing pro ball in Europe has become attractive to players from throughout the world, and in this regard, Albania is very much a part of Europe. A look at the roster of any BFA team will show that Albanian basketball includes players from Albania and throughout the world, including many North Americans from such places as Missouri and California.

Like organized basketball in North America, the BFA holds playoffs that culminate in a national championship. As with soccer, however, in Albania, girls' and women's basketball has not achieved the acceptance or success that it has at the school, college, and professional levels in North America.

In addition to scheduling games against teams from other European nations through EuroBasket, the BFA

These ethnic Albanian boys from Kosovo live in a refugee camp in the city of Kukes.

also has a close working relationship with organized basketball in Kosovo, the embattled region in Serbia and Montenegro with which Albania shares both a border and political, social, religious, and ethnic ties. Because of tensions in Kosovo between ethnic Albanians and Serbia and Montenegro's primarily Serbian government, organized basketball in that region operates, for now, under the terms of a United Nations peace agreement and looks to Albania as a source of support and competitive play.

Fatmir Vata is a midfielder with the Albanian national team.

SOCCER

Like fans throughout the rest of Europe, Albanians love soccer more than any other sport. The history of the game in Albania in many ways mirrors the nation's own development in the 20th century.

Known to most of the world as football, soccer was probably brought to Albania by Christian missionaries in the early 1900s, when Albania was under Ottoman rule. Following World War I, British troops stationed in Albania helped make the game more popular, encouraging Albanians to develop local teams of their own.

Albanian soccer teams began playing teams from other nations in the early 1920s and formed their own football federation in 1930. From 1930 on, every major city and town had its own football league. World War II resulted in a break from international and national competition. But in 1944–45, football teams once again took to the fields in competition for a national championship. Albania was soon playing national teams from other countries and in 1946 hosted the Balkan Cup tournament of teams from throughout the region.

By 1953, however, Albania had become increasingly closed off due to the policies of its new communist government. Despite becoming a member of the Union of European Football Associations (UEFA) in 1954, from November 1953 until June 1963, the Albanian national team played only two international football matches, one in 1957 against the People's Republic of China and one in 1958 against East Germany. Throughout this period the Albanian government continued to support soccer programs at the state, school, and local levels, and Albanians continued to play soccer—but mostly within their own borders in local leagues and for teams playing in Albanian national competitions. In a few instances, talented Albanian players fled their homeland to play for teams in other nations, notably Italy.

In the 1960s Albanian soccer reentered the international arena. Its national team appeared in the 1964 Olympics, the 1964 and 1968 European Championship Games, and the 1966 World Cup. In the early 1970s Albania improved its performance in international competition and in the 1980s entered its first international tournament under the auspices of the prestigious UEFA.

Since the end of communist restrictions on emigration in the early 1990s, Albanians have watched many of their nation's most talented players leave for the chance to play in other countries. They have also had their hopes for the national team's success in Europe—and ultimately the World Cup—raised, lowered, and raised again by a succession of coaches from Italy and Germany.

Meanwhile, Albanians continue to follow—and, if they are males, to play—soccer in their cities and towns. The Albanian Football Federation sponsors league play on several levels, and fans throughout the nation follow their favorite teams in the Football Federation's First Division, a league of between ten and fourteen teams in the major cities that compete against one another for the national championship.

Unlike most other nations in Europe, Albania has done little to encourage participation in soccer among girls, and the nation does not field women's teams in national or international competition.

Mancaku from Albania (left) tries to keep the ball from Ganayem of Israel during a match in Tirana.

TENNIS

In the 1930s tennis became suddenly popular in Albania as students returning from France, Italy, and other Western European countries brought tennis back with them. Tirana and most other major Albanian cities built public tennis courts, and Albania even competed against other nations in international events.

In the 1950s, however, the public was banned from playing tennis by Albania's communist government, claiming it was a bourgeois sport that was suited only to privileged members of the upper classes in capitalist countries. Most public courts were neglected and fell into disrepair, and Albanians were not allowed to compete in international events. Still, people who worked for the government were allowed to keep playing tennis, and for their pleasure some of the courts were kept in good shape.

For years Albania was still mostly a no-show at international tennis organizations and events. In 1985, however, the Albanian Tennis Federation was created. Now, with a national tennis association to promote the sport and create a calendar of regular matches and tournaments, the sport has been brought back to life across the country. In the 1990s Albania struggled to find the funds to keep its courts in playable condition. In 1996 Albania took a huge step in the development of tennis as a national sport. The Albanian Tennis Federation joined the International Tennis Federation and the European Tennis Federation, opening the door for Albanians to compete in European and world tournaments. Since then, tennis has been flourishing in many parts of the country, especially in Tirana, where the Tirana Tennis School developed a relationship with a tennis school in Bari, Italy. In 1999 the schools in Tirana and Bari began an exchange program, with coaches and players sharing their tennis experience with one another and scheduling matches between the two schools.

TAKING TENNIS BACK TO THE PEOPLE

In the early years of its becoming a communist state following World War II, Albania began to isolate itself from the rest of the world, withdrawing increasingly within its own borders and excluding its citizens from the kinds of activities that were allowed even by other communist nations in Europe. Sports activities were no exception, and for years Albanians were restricted even in the kinds of games they could play.

During the 1950s, Albania's government prohibited most of its citizens from playing tennis, claiming that the sport was more suited to the privileged upper classes of Western capitalist nations than to the working-class members of a communist state like Albania. Most of Albania's tennis players disappeared from its public tennis courts, which had became neglected and overgrown with weeds, and Albania disappeared from the world of international tennis.

Since 1990 Albania has come roaring back to life in the world of international tennis. It joined both the European Tennis Federation and the International Tennis Federation (ITF) in 1996. Albanian teams are competing in international matches, and now the Albanian Tennis Federation is making a huge effort to bring tennis back to the people, especially children, through various programs in Albania's cities and schools.

TENNIS IN THE SQUARE

The Albanian Tennis Federation is also developing a program called Tennis in the Square to encourage people to learn and play tennis in Albania's larger cities. Experienced players set up programs in the main city square and teach basic techniques to children. The project also donates tennis equipment to local sports clubs and encourages them to open "mini-courts" for children.

Although the reach of these tennis programs is limited by lack of funding and qualified personnel, they do possess certain strengths that should help make them successful: enthusiasm and vision. The goal of both Tennis in Schools (*opposite, sidebar*) and Tennis in the Square is to foster a love for the sport in children at a young age.

And Tennis in the Square has a goal that sets it apart even from programs in other, wealthier nations—to bring the same tennis programs being developed in Albania to children in neighboring Kosovo, the war-ravaged province of Serbia and Montenegro whose people share ethnic, cultural, and familial ties with Albanians.

Satellite dishes are a common sight in Albania, indicative of how popular television is among the Albanian people.

TELEVISION

Watching television is a very popular pastime in Albania, as it is in many other parts of the world. Satellite TV, even under communist rule, brought shows from places outside the country. Today, people rely on it to escape the somewhat dull fare available locally and to draw in the glamorous shows from Italy and other parts of Europe. Albanians jokingly refer to their TV set as a member of the family.

Troc is a weekly television show aimed at young people and seen by over 90 percent of children between the ages of 11 and 15. Coproduced by Albanian National Television and UNICEF in a newsmagazine format, it introduces children to the importance of dialogue, debate, and fact gathering. Since over half of Albania's young people say they plan to emigrate, one goal of the program is to illuminate the needs of and opportunities in Albania, with the hope that children will commit themselves to their homeland. The key to *Troc*'s success is that the news segments, eight each week from around the country, are chosen, written, and produced by young people from 15 to 18 years of age. Some of the stories stimulate activism, but others celebrate the beauty and traditions of Albania. The young people working on the show also gain technical expertise with state of the art equipment. They learn to shoot, edit, interview, and write.

With so much television coming from Italy and the United States, many Albanian broadcasters attempt to imitate their style. *Troc* is a refreshing change and a uniquely Albanian program that even adults think sets an example that local stations should follow.

For many Albanians, the television set is like a member of the family.

SCOUTING AND OTHER OUTDOOR SPORTING ACTIVITIES

Albania's beautiful natural settings have given Albanians a wide range of sporting activities. Like children everywhere, Albanian boys and girls play many outdoor games, including skipping rope, hide-and-seek, tag, and volleyball. In fact, volleyball is popular enough that people of all ages play volleyball indoors, primarily in the major cities.

Swimming in the Adriatic Sea is a popular summer activity, as are fishing and boating in both the Adriatic and Albania's many inland lakes. With its varied terrain Albania is a popular place for hikers and mountain climbers.

The city of Durres lies on the Adriatic coast and is an ideal beach location for both Albanians and tourists to the country.

Mountain climbing has attracted women in particular, and mountain-climbing races are a traditional Albanian sport for women.

As Albania has become more fully a member of the European family of nations one activity with widespread international appeal has become increasingly popular among Albanian children—scouting.

In many ways Albania's relationship with scouting parallels its relationship with other international organizations. A member of the World Organization of the Scouting Movement (WOSM) from 1920 until 1937, Albania entered a dark age in its involvement in scouting through World War II and beyond. In the 1990s, with reforms instituted by the new government, scouting was reestablished, and in 1999 Albania became once again a member of the WOSM. As in WOSM groups worldwide, both boys and girls participated in what once was known as the Boy Scouts.

In 1998, with help from Italian Guides and Scouts representatives, the Association of Guides and Scouts in Albania was founded with much enthusiasm for both the activities the group offers and the chance for Albanian girls and young women to participate in international scouting events.

Today, the Albanian Association of Guides and Scouts performs environmental cleanup campaigns and other social services and introduces its members to many forms of outdoor recreation. The Association of Guides and Scouts is mostly for girls, but like the Boy Scouts, it includes members of both sexes in its programs.

Members of the Beslidh-ja Scout Albania (BSA), the association of scouts and guides in Albania.

FESTIVALS

ALBANIA HAS SEVERAL fixed national holidays, but when its system of government changed, some that had been official were dropped. Today, the legal holidays are New Year's Day, which is celebrated on January 1; International Labor Day, May 1; Independence Day, November 28; and Christmas Day, December 25. Additionally, the day of the elections for the People's Assembly is a national holiday, whenever it occurs. Besides the fixed holidays there are three important movable holidays. Though they are not necessarily celebrated by closing government offices and businesses, these are the holidays that Albanians hold most important.

Opposite and below: **To celebrate International Labor Day on May 1, Albania's workforce comes out in full force to participate in a parade in the capital city of Tirana.**

MUSLIM HOLIDAYS

Two of the movable holidays are Muslim holy days—the first day of Ramadan, which begins a month of fasting, and the end of the fasting period, Eid al-Fitr. The dates for these holy days are fixed by the lunar calendar, which has only 354 days, so their dates fall eleven days earlier each year according to the Gregorian calendar. The Gregorian calendar is based on the solar year, which is approximately 365 days.

The first day of Ramadan marks the beginning of a period of fasting, prayer, and introspection. Observant Muslims fast from sunrise to sundown, taking neither food nor drink until after dark. The end of the fasting is celebrated on Eid al-Fitr, also called Small Bayram, when families, friends, and whole communities come together to sing and dance, play traditional music, and, of course, feast on food prepared according to old family recipes. The celebrations continue long into the night, propelled by stories the old folks heard from their parents.

Albanian Muslim men gather for prayers in Tirana's Skenderbeg Square, in celebration of Eid al-Fitr.

CHRISTIAN HOLIDAYS

Albanian Christians celebrate Christmas and Easter like Christians all over the world with family gatherings and special church services. Because it is a national holiday, even non-Christians have large family gatherings on Christmas. The people of Tirana hold a music festival as well at Christmastime, during which local and international musicians perform traditional and classical music to large crowds. Increasingly, this festival includes performances of cutting-edge music by young musicians who have been influenced by international trends.

Christians light candles
in a church on Christmas
morning.

EASTER

The third movable holiday is Easter, which is the holiest of Christian holidays and is marked by solemn processions to churches in villages and cities throughout the country. Red eggs are important to Albanian Christians at Easter, and people will dye them and tap them gently against their friends's eggs in greeting. In communities where religious differences are not taken too seriously, Muslims and Christians also exchange eggs. Women traditionally dye enough eggs to give to anyone who calls at their house between Maundy Thursday, the day before the crucifixion, and Ascension, which is celebrated 40 days after Easter.

If a young woman is to be married during the Easter season, her future mother-in-law will give her an egg and a candle at the Easter service. The gift is to assure her fertility.

123

Albanian children, in their national costume, wave the nation's flag in celebration of the country's Independence Day on November 28.

FAMILY AND COMMUNITY CELEBRATIONS

Albanians have traditionally had large families and have celebrated family milestones in festive gatherings. Weddings, births, funerals, and birthdays are all cause for people to sing, dance, tell stories, and eat traditional foods prepared as they have been through generations.

Dance and music festivals occur throughout the country, especially in the warmer weather when they can be held outdoors. The isolation of Albanians, especially in the mountains, has had the fortunate effect of preserving traditions in dance and music for centuries. Until after World War II, in fact, traditional music was the only music Albanians knew. Under the rule of the Communists, much of this music was recorded and preserved in archives. At the same time, the government introduced the people to Western music and trained classical musicians. Today, Albanians in the cities are exposed to a richness of music, both traditional and classical.

At weddings and music and dance festivals, Albanians welcome the opportunity to wear the costumes that represent their traditional garb. As recently as 1940, these were not costumes at all for many, but daily dress. Though the country is tiny, the costumes are varied and unique to each location. Like the music, the costumes reflect the influence of Albania's invaders.

In the city of Tropoja, for example, men dress in a close-fitting white skullcap and loose white shirt. A short vest, black in front and red in the back, goes over the shirt. Low-slung black trousers are held up by a complex series of sashes, one white, the others colored and elaborately fringed. Women also wear a snowy white shirt topped with a short vest. A long white skirt with a bright red apron completes the outfit.

In Tirana, the white skullcap is still the first identifying mark of the Albanian man. Like his countrymen to the north, he wears the white shirt and black pants. His vest, though, is heavily embroidered and distinctive. The woman's vest also is uniquely decorated, often with the same motifs and colors as the man's. She may wear a small hat that coordinates with her vest, or she may have her head completely covered in the Muslim tradition by a shawl. Her long white skirt will be covered in front by a large, beautifully embroidered apron, and her long-sleeved blouse will proclaim the artistry of her mother or herself in a color and design that are her family's alone.

In southern Albania, the man's white skullcap is slightly larger, more like a Turkish fez, but still identifiably Albanian. The white shirt is still there as well, as is the short vest. But instead of the black trousers, the man wears a short, full white skirt over tight white pants or leggings. Women wear bright, embroidered skirts, aprons, and vests. In Dropull, women may wear a headpiece composed of a lacy, white, tiara-shaped hat and a shoulder-length veil. Their white skirts and blouses are topped with one-piece embroidered aprons that cover both their blouse fronts and their skirts.

The elements of the Albanian costume have symbolic meaning. The black vest, the *xhokia e zeze* (joh-KEE-ah eh ZEH-zeh), for example, represents the mourning of the Albanian people for the death of George Skenderbeg, their national hero. Various forms of men's trousers can indicate vassalage under tyranny. When dancers and singers wear their costumes, they add a visual significance to their performance that goes beyond their music and movements.

The passion of the Glory is the dominant characteristic of the Albanians. Their genius is poetic as their customs; their popular songs, above all those of the heroic age of Skenderbeg, remember Homer's songs . . . they fuse, like Achilles, the poetry with music and dance. Their feudal organization (the code of the Mountains) does not lessen at all the feeling of general freedom and the patriotic passion, the noblest patrimony of the Albanians.

—Alphonse de LaMartine

FOOD

THE CULINARY TRADITIONS of Italy, Turkey, and Greece have combined in Albania to create a unique cuisine. The Mediterranean climate makes it possible to grow figs, olives, grapes, and most vegetables. Sheep and cattle adjust well to the mountainous terrain, and herbs and spices thrive along the coasts. Fish and other seafood abound in the Adriatic and Ionian seas.

ALBANIAN FOOD

Vegetables and fruits in Albania are especially delicious. They are all grown organically, not because of environmental virtue, but because neither the government nor the farmers can afford to use fertilizers or pesticides that are chemical based. Favorite vegetables in summer include eggplant, green beans, and okra. In winter, cabbages, carrots, and potatoes, all vegetables that keep well, are featured in stews and soups. Electricity limitations keep people from freezing food, and poor roads inhibit shipping, so many Albanians eat seasonally and locally. In the winter, for example, people make salads from pickled vegetables such as cucumbers, peppers, and eggplant.

Lamb is Albania's most popular meat. Often it is spit roasted, especially in restaurants, where it is sliced off for use in sandwiches. Economic constraints as well as preference mean that Albanians eat as much of the lamb as they can, including heart, liver, brains, kidneys, and whatever organs there are left. One Albanian specialty is *pace koke* (PAH-seh KOH-keh), a breakfast soup made from the sheep's head.

Above: **In the Dajti mountains near Tirana, an Albanian man barbecues a whole lamb on a spit.**

Opposite: **A shop in Tirana with a range of food items for sale.**

127

An Albanian family share a simple meal.

THE ALBANIAN MEAL

Albanian cooks stretch their food, especially meat, in other ways as well. Chopped meat provides the protein in many meals, stuffed into cabbage leaves, peppers, potatoes, and zucchini. Yogurt and cheese are also used to make meat go further. One dish, *turli* (TOOR-lih), layers any vegetable the cook has available with tomatoes and simmers them all with a cut of veal to serve the whole family. In Albania, veal is the meat of a calf that is allowed to grow for a longer time, and to a larger size, to produce more meat than in most other countries.

A main meal on Sunday or for guests might typically include an appetizer or salad, a main meal, and a dessert and coffee. Most of what Albanians eat will be what is locally available because shipping throughout the country adds so much to the cost. The first course might consist of tomatoes, either with or without vinegar, and a chewy bread that is dipped in warm, thick yogurt. The main meal could be chicken, beef, mutton, or fish. Along the Adriatic or Ionian coasts, there is a wide variety of fish, but inland it is most likely to be carp, a fish that feeds on the bottom of the river. Noodles accompany many entrées.

Dessert is often fruit, mostly figs or prunes, or crème caramel, an egg custard topped with caramelized sugar.

ALBANIAN DRINKS

Beverages include bottled or boiled water, Turkish coffee, wine, and raki, the Albanian brandy that outsiders might mistake for liquid flame. There is also Italian beer and a beer made by the Tirana brewery. A fondness for the Tirana beer can be acquired, but many Albanians have not acquired it.

Albanian wines are often very good. The Korce region produces a Merlot and a Tokay. An indigenous Albanian grape is responsible for the Berati Kabernet and Kallmet from the northern city of Shkodra.

El Chicco Kafe is a coffee liquer produced in Albania.

The traditional alcoholic drink is raki, a clear liquor usually made from grapes, although Albanians also make it from mulberries or plums. It is most often drunk by men in the morning, but it is also considered a digestive aid, and can be drunk just about anytime at all.

But most commonly, the drink of choice is coffee, traditionally *kafe turke* (KAH-feh turk), Turkish coffee. In Albanian homes in the villages and countryside, kafe turke is what will be served to guests. It is made by combining finely ground coffee, water, and sugar in one pot and boiling it till it is ready. Served in small cups, kafe turke provides the proper atmosphere for arranging marriages, making deals, and resolving disagreements short of a blood feud. In the cities, coffee is most often prepared in Italian espresso machines.

BYREK

Byrek (BIH-rek) is a dish known as *burek* by Serbs, *spanakopita* by Greeks, and other names by other ethnic groups in the region. Its required ingredient is phyllo dough, but beyond that the makings can vary widely from culture to culture and, within Albania, from household to household. Byrek can be stuffed with spinach and cheese or with meat, usually lamb, and eggs and nuts. It can be shaped like a pie or made into individual small triangles. Following is one variety that shows the influence of several cultures, the mint of the Turks, the cheeses of the Italians, and the phyllo dough of Greece. But it is all Albanian.

8 tablespoons butter
1 package frozen phyllo dough
5 eggs
16 ounces (454 g) ricotta cheese

16 ounces (454 g) feta cheese
8 ounces (227 g) Romano cheese
8 ounces (227 g) fresh dill
Dried herbs: mint, oregano, thyme

Thaw the phyllo dough at least 2 hours. If it is even slightly frozen, wait till it thaws. Unfold and cover with a damp towel. Mix all the filling ingredients together until smooth and creamy. Melt ½ cup butter, and spread about 1 tablespoon of it on the bottom of a 9-inch round cake pan. Carefully separate the sheets of phyllo dough, and layer them in the bottom of the pan. Brush each sheet with butter as you lay it in. Leave half of each sheet hanging out of the pan. Pour the filling into the pan. Fold the hanging sheets over the top of the filling to cover the pie. Brush with more butter. Bake at 375°F (190°C) for 45 minutes or until it is brown and crisp. Remove from the oven and the pan, and let set for 10 minutes. Slice into pie-shaped pieces and serve.

QOFTE

Another popular dish in Albania is *qofte* (CHOH-ftee). In the Middle East, it is often known as *cubby* or *kufta*. It is cooked at home, in restaurants, or on the street. It can be baked or fried, served with salad and French fries, or with seasoned yogurt or tomato sauce. This is one recipe for it, but there are as many others as there are cooks.

1 pound (16 ounces / 454 g) lamb or beef, ground
8 ounces (227 g) chopped onion
2 ounces (57 g) breadcrumbs
2 ounces (57 g) feta cheese, crumbled
1 clove crushed garlic

2 ounces (57 g) fresh mint
½ teaspoon cinnamon
½ teaspoon oregano
Salt and pepper
Flour and oil

Mix all the ingredients except for the flour and oil. Let flavors blend for one hour. Then shape into eight sausage-like cylinders, roll in flour, and fry for about 8 minutes in heated oil, turning two or three times. You can serve these as appetizers. They are especially good dipped in a sauce made from yogurt, garlic, and chopped mint. As a main course, it can be served with rice or buttered noodles.

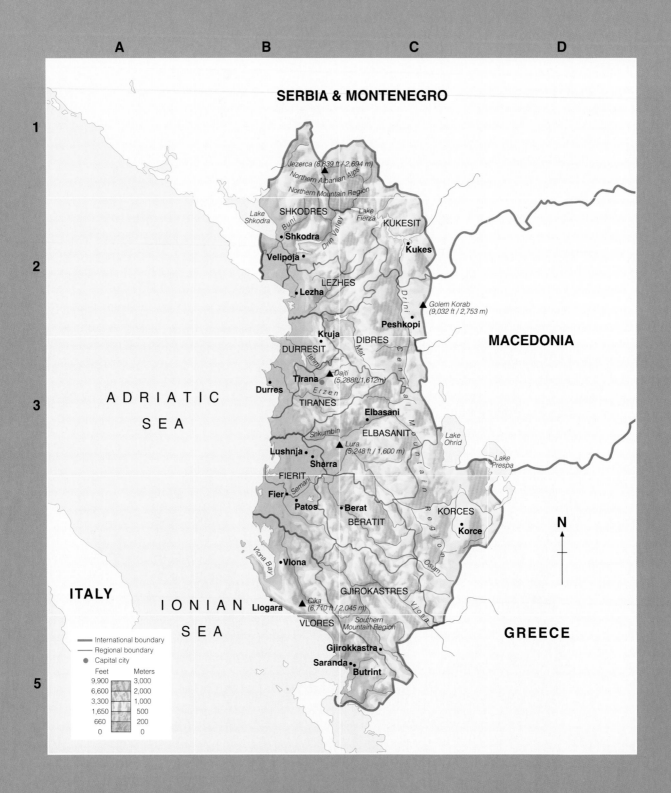

SERBIA & MONTENEGRO

A   B   C   D

1

Jezerca (8,839 ft / 2,694 m)
Northern Albanian Alps
Northern Mountain Region

SHKODRES
Lake Shkodra   *Lake Fierza*
• Shkodra   **KUKESIT**

• Velipoja   **• Kukes**

2

LEZHES
• Lezha

Drini ▲ Golem Korab
(9,032 ft / 2,753 m)

Kruja   **• Peshkopi**

DURRESIT   **DIBRES**

Ishm   ▲ *Dajti*
Tirana   *(5,288ft/1,612m)*
• Durres   *Erzen*

TIRANES   **• Elbasani**

3

ELBASANIT
Shkumbin   *Lake Ohrid*

• Lushnja   ▲ *Lura*   *Lake Prespa*
(5,248 ft / 1,600 m)
• Sharra

FIERIT
Semani
• Fier   **KORCES**
• Patos   **• Berat**

BERATIT   **• Korce**

N

A D R I A T I C

S E A

Vlora Bay
• Vlona   *Osum*

ITALY   ▲ *Cika*
I O N I A N   *(6,710 ft / 2,045 m)*
• Llogara   **GJIROKASTRES**
S E A
VLORES   *Southern Mountain Region*

• Gjirokkastra

• Saranda
• Butrint

MACEDONIA

GREECE

Central Mountain Region

Vjosa

Legend:
— International boundary
— Regional boundary
● Capital city

Feet	Meters
9,900	3,000
6,600	2,000
3,300	1,000
1,650	500
660	200
0	0

5

MAP OF ALBANIA

ECONOMIC ALBANIA

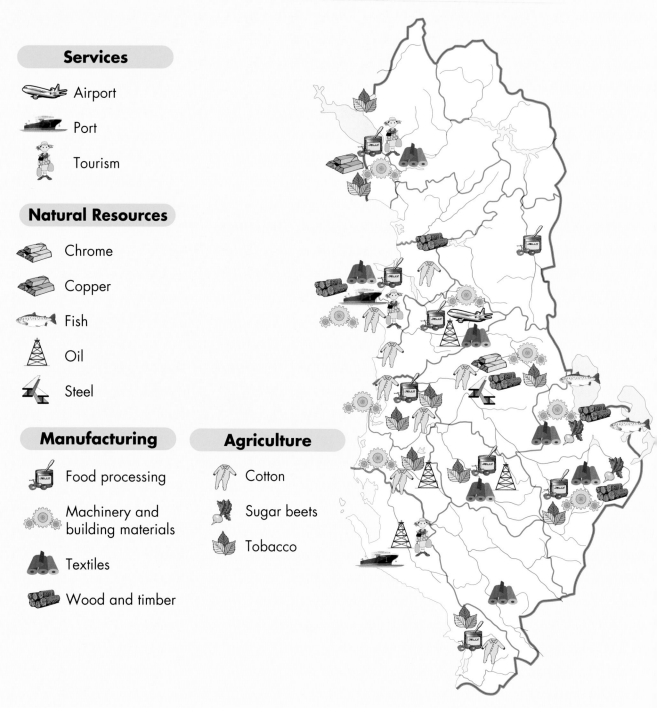

Services

- Airport
- Port
- Tourism

Natural Resources

- Chrome
- Copper
- Fish
- Oil
- Steel

Manufacturing

- Food processing
- Machinery and building materials
- Textiles
- Wood and timber

Agriculture

- Cotton
- Sugar beets
- Tobacco

ABOUT
THE ECONOMY

OVERVIEW
Albania is one of the poorest countries in Europe. The transition from a communist system to an open-market economy has been difficult. The current government continues to institute policies that curb violent crime and energize economic activity and trade. Foreign aid, mostly from Greece and Italy ($400–600 million annually) helps offset the trade deficit. In addition, the country still relies on Albanians working in Greece, Italy, and Germany who send financial support home. Agriculture, which accounts for 34 percent of the GDP, is hindered by frequent drought, antiquated machinery, poor management, lack of incentives for farmers, and the persistence of traditional farming methods. Inadequate energy infrastructure further impedes economic growth. The government continues efforts to improve Albania's limited transportation systems.

NATURAL RESOURCES
Petroleum, natural gas, coal, bauxite, chromite, copper, iron ore, nickel, salt, timber, hydropower

CURRENCY
1 Albanian lek (ALL) = 100 qintars
USD 1 = ALL 121.8 (2003 est.)
Notes: 100, 200, 500, 1000, 5,000 lek
Coins: 5, 10, 20, 50, 100 lek

INDUSTRIAL PRODUCTS
Food processing, textiles and clothing, lumber, oil, cement, chemicals, mining, basic metals, hydropower

AGRICULTURE PRODUCTS
Wheat, corn, potatoes, sugar beets, grapes, meat, dairy products

MAJOR EXPORTS
Textiles and footwear, asphalt, metals and metallic ores, crude oil, vegetables, fruits, tobacco

EXPORT PARTNERS
Italy, Greece, Germany

MAJOR IMPORTS
Machinery and equipment, foodstuffs, textiles, chemicals

IMPORT PARTNERS
Italy, Greece, Turkey, Germany

LABOUR DISTRTIBUTION
Agriculture 50 percent, industry 27 percent, services 23 percent

EMPLOYMENT RATE
70 percent

PORTS AND HARBORS
Durres, Saranda, Shengjin, Vlona

AIRPORTS
11 total; 3 with paved runways

CULTURAL ALBANIA

Rozafa Castle
Located in Shkodra, the Rozafa Castle was built in Illyrian times. The castle was erected as a fortress with still extant vaults, tunnels, courtyards, and walls. It was the last of Skenderbeg's citadels to fall to the Turks in 1479.

Skenderbeg's Burial Site
Lezha is the place where Skenderbeg united the Albanian tribal chieftains in their 25-year stand-off of the Ottoman empire. It is also the site of his burial in the cathedral.

Religious Center
Durres is the seat of both the bishop of the Greek Orthodox church and the archbishop of the Roman Catholic church. Just outside the city are the remains of a 2nd century Byzantine amphitheater—the largest in the Balkans—and 5th century Venetian city walls.

Skenderbeg Museum
Situated in Kruja, the Skenderbeg Museum was initially the ancestral home of George Skenderbeg. It was the center of the Albanian resistance during the Ottoman invasion.

Proclamation Site
Vlona is the place where the Adriatic and Ionian Seas divide. The city is also the site where Albanian independence was proclaimed in 1912.

National Historical Museum
Located in Tirana, the capital city and seat of government, this museum house historical and cultural artifacts that have been collected to tell the story of Albania from prehistoric times through communism.

Petrela Castle
This castle in Elbasani was a key defensive site of Skenderbeg's troops in the 15th century. Elbasani means "place for raiding other people's lands."

"Museum City"
The communists designated Berat a "museum city," therefore leaving many of its mosques and medieval churches and icons intact.

National Museum of Medieval Art
This museum in Korce boasts of collections of icons from 16 centuries.

Ethnographic Museum
This house in Gjirokkastra was the birthplace of Enver Hoxha. In recent years, it was transformed into the Ethnographic Museum.

Roman Ruins
Butrint is the site of an urban center in the 4th century, a roman theater and bath house, and other archaeological riches.

Religious Artifacts
The coastal town of Saranda has yielded the remains of a Christian Basilica dating back to the 5th and 6th centuries, multicolored mosaics, and a Christian Monastery. Saranda is now part of the Albanian Riviera.

ABOUT THE CULTURE

OFFICIAL COUNTRY NAME
Republika e Shqiperise, short form: Shqiperia.
English translation: Republic of Albania

FLAG DESCRIPTION
Red with a black, two-headed eagle at the center

CAPITAL
Tirana

ADMINISTRATIVE DIVISIONS
12 counties: Beratit, Dibres, Durresit, Elbasanit, Fierit, Gjirokastres, Korces, Kukesit, Lezhes, Shkodres, Tiranes, Vlores

POPULATION
3,544,808 (July 2004 est.)

ETHNIC GROUPS
Albanian, Bulgarian, Greek, Macedonian, Roma (Gypsy), Serb, Vlach

BIRTH RATE
15.08 births per 1,000 population (2004 est.)

DEATH RATE
5.02 deaths per 1,000 population (2004 est.)

NET MIGRATION RATE
-4.93 migrant(s) per 1,000 population (2004 est.)

RELIGIONS
Albanian Orthodox, Muslim, Roman Catholic

LANGUAGES
Shqip (Albanian), Greek

LITERACY RATE
86.5 percent

HOLIDAYS
New Year's Day (January 1–2), Nevruz Day (March 22), Catholic Easter (April 20), Orthodox Easter (April 27); May Day (May 1), Mother Teresa Day (October 19), Independence Day (November 28), Liberation Day (November 29), Christmas Day (December 25), Small Bayram and Big Bayram (date varies according to the Islamic calendar)

LEADERS IN POLITICS
Enver Hoxha—Communist dictator
King Zog I (Ahmed Bey Zogu)—20th century king
    of Albania
Alfred Moisiu—president since July 2002
Fatos Nano—prime minister since July 2002

OTHER IMPORTANT ALBANIANS
Skenderbeg (George Kastrioti)—15th century hero
Ismail Kadare—contemporary writer
Fan S. Noli—Albanian writer, priest, premier from
    1880–1865

TIME LINE

IN ALBANIA	IN THE WORLD
1225 B.C. Illyrians establish themselves in Albania.	**753 B.C.** Rome is founded.
400–300 B.C. Illyrian kingdom reaches it peak of power.	
165 B.C. Rome captures Albania.	**116–17 B.C.** The Roman Empire reaches its greatest extent, under Emperor Trajan (98–17).
A.D. 732 Illyrian lands come under rule of Constantinople.	**A.D. 600** Height of Mayan civilization. **1000** The Chinese perfect gunpowder and begin to use it in warfare.
1389 Ottomans take over some Albanian lands.	
1443 George Skenderbeg mounts resistance to Turks and holds them at bay for next 20 years.	
1479 Ottoman rule becomes complete and last for 400 years.	**1530** Beginning of trans-Atlantic slave trade organized by the Portuguese in Africa. **1558–1603** Reign of Elizabeth I of England.
1600–1800 Albania becomes a Muslim land as two-thirds of the people convert to Islam.	**1620** Pilgrims sail the *Mayflower* to America. **1776** U.S. Declaration of Independence. **1789–1799** The French Revolution. **1861** The U.S. Civil War begins. **1869** The Suez Canal is opened.
1912 Albanians declare Albania independent and establish provision government.	**1914** World War I begins.

IN ALBANIA	IN THE WORLD
1928 Albania becomes a kingdom under King Zog.	
1940 Italy annexes Albania.	**1939** World War II begins.
1941 Albanian Communist Party founded under Enver Hoxha.	
1944 Albania forms a communist government.	**1945** The United States drops atomic bombs on Hiroshima and Nagasaki.
	1949 The North Atlantic Treaty Organization (NATO) is formed.
	1957 The Russians launch Sputnik.
	1966–1969 The Chinese Cultural Revolution.
1985 Hoxha dies, succeeded by Ramiz Alia, who continues Hoxha's policies and practices.	**1986** Nuclear power disaster at Chernobyl in Ukraine.
1990 Demonstrations result in liberalizing of government.	**1991** Break-up of the Soviet Union.
1991 First multiparty elections held in 50 years, Alia is re-elected and communist constitution is thrown out.	
1997 Government-led pyramid scheme collapses. Albanian people riot.	**1997** Hong Kong is returned to China.
1999 Refugees from Kosovo flee to Albania for refuge from NATO bombs.	**2001** Terrorists crash planes in New York, Washington, D.C., and Pennsylvania.
2004 Albania declares the year of Mother Teresa.	**2003** War in Iraq.

GLOSSARY

besa (BEH-sah)
An Albanian's word of honor, strongly held even to the point of blood feud.

balkanize
To knowingly assemble a group of people who have differing, usually incompatible, goals.

byrek (BIH-rek)
A pie made from phyllo dough and various stuffings such as spinach, cheese, and lamb.

Eid al-Fitr
The Muslim celebration of the end of Ramadan, a time of feasting, music, and gathering of friends and families.

Gheg (or Geg)
The people of northern Albania; the dialect of Shqip, the Albanian language, spoken there and in Kosovo, Macedonia, and Montenegro.

kafe turke (KAH-feh turk)
Albanian coffee, made from boiled water, coffee, and sugar.

kalashnikov
A Soviet assault rifle capable of firing many bullets with one pull of the trigger.

lahuta (LAH-hoo-tah)
An Albanian stringed instrument, similar to the lute, today used to accompany singers, but traditionally used by poets to call people to hear their recitations.

pasha
A local ruling representative of the Ottoman Empire.

pace koke (PAH-seh KOH-keh)
A breakfast soup made from the meat of a sheep's head.

pyramid scheme
A fraudulent get-rich-quick plan whereby a few early investors at the top of the pyramid take the money of many later investors at the bottom of the pyramid who lose everything.

qofti (CHOH-ftee)
Albanian meatballs or uncased sausages.

raki (RAH-kee)
An alcoholic drink, similar to brandy, made and served in Albanian homes as well as commercially.

Ramadan
A monthlong period of fasting and prayer for Muslims, observed variously in the late winter or early spring.

Shqip
The Albanian language, a language unrelated to any other known language, spoken by Albanians in countries all over the world.

Tosk
Albanians from southern Albania and the dialect they and Greek Albanians speak of their language, Shqip.

FURTHER INFORMATION

BOOKS

Elsie, Robert. *The Dictionary of Albanian Religion, Mythology, and Folk Culture*. New York: New York University Press, 2000.

Kadare, Ismail. *Broken April*. New York: New Amsterdam Books, 1998.

Lear, Aaron. *Albania* (Major World Nations). Chelsea House, 2000.

Lerner Geography Department. *Albania in Pictures* (Visual Geography). Minneapolis: Lerner, 1995

Sherer, Stan, and Marjorie Senechal. *Long Life to Your Children: A Portrait of High Albania*. Amherst, MA: University of Massachusetts Press, 1997.

Tomas, Jason. *King Zog of Albania: Europe's Self-made Muslim Monarch*. New York: New York University Press, 2004.

Vickers, Miranda. *The Albanians: A Modern History*. London: I.B. Tauris, 2001.

Wright, David K. *Albania* (Enchantment of the World Second Series). Children's Press, 1997.

WEBSITES

BBC Country Profile. news.bbc.co.uk/1/hi/world/Europe/country_profiles/1004234.stm

Central Intelligence Agency World Factbook (select "Albania") from the country list).

Home of Albanians Online. www.albanian.com/community/index.php

Lonely Planet Guide. www.lonelyplanet.com/destinations/Europe/Albania

Library of Congress Country Study. lcweb2.loc.gov/frd/cs/altoc.html

The United Nations Development Programme : Albania. www.undp.org.al

Virutal Albanian Online. www.albania.8m.com

Words without Borders. www.wordswithoutborders.org

MUSIC

Albanian Village Music. Heritage Music, 1998.

Folk Music of Albania. Topic Records, 1994.

Music from Albania: (Anthology of World Music). Rounder, 1999.

Songs and Dances from Albania. Tirana Folk Ensemble. Arc Music, 2000

Vocal Traditions of Albania. Saydisc, 2000.

VIDEOS

Come Home Alive: State of Emergency: Albania. History Channel, 1997.

BIBLIOGRAPHY

Ash, Timothy Garton. *History of the Present: Essays, Sketches, and Dispatches from Europe in the 1990s.* New York: Random House, 1999.

Brown, James, F. *Hopes and Shadows: Eastern Europe After Communism.* Durham: Duke University Press, 1994.

D'Aluisio, Faith and Peter Menzel. *Women in the Material World.* San Francisco: Sierra Club Books, 1996.

Gloyer, Gillian. *Albania: The Bradt Travel Guide.* Guilford, Connecticut: Pequot Press, 2004.

Newall, Venetia. *An Egg at Easter: Folklore Study.* Boston: Routledge and Kegan Paul, 1971.

West, Rebecca. *Black Lamb and Grey Falcon: A Journey through Yugoslavia.* New York: Penguin, 1940.

Winchester, Simon. *The Fracture Zone: A Return to the Balkans.* New York: Harper Collins, 1999.

INDEX